999

999

MICHAEL BUERK

DRAMATIC STORIES
OF REAL-LIFE RESCUES

BBC BOOKS

ALL THE **999 SAFETY ADVICE** GIVEN IN THIS BOOK HAS BEEN APPROVED BY MEMBERS OF THE RELEVANT SAFETY ORGANIZATIONS.

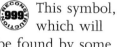 This symbol, which will be found by some captions, indicates that the photograph was taken during the filming of the reconstruction of the story. Some of the photos therefore show the actors playing the parts of the individuals featured in the stories, while others show the individuals themselves taking part in the filming of their own stories.

ACKNOWLEDGEMENTS

There are many people I need to thank. Television is a collective business; the programme, and now the book, depends on the skills and hard work of the 999 team. To the researchers and directors who found these stories and turned them into gripping television, I owe a considerable debt. Andrea Brown's organizational abilities and stamina are entirely responsible for the 999 Safety Advice sections. The book would not have been written without the vision and enthusiasm of 999's producer, Andy Batten-Foster, the man ultimately responsible for the programme's success. He has been patient and tolerant, but then people who tell such awful jokes have to be; there is no nicer man in television.

Above all, this book is dedicated to Britain's emergency services. Some of those whose courage is described in these stories were there by accident. The courage of the men and women of the emergency services is on call, twenty-four hours a day.

This book is published to accompany the television series entitled 999

Published by BBC Books, a division of BBC Enterprises Limited, Woodlands, 80 Wood Lane, London W12 0TT

First Published 1994

© Michael Buerk 1994

ISBN 0 563 37049 1

Illustrations by Ali Marshall

Set in Joanna by Ace Filmsetting Ltd, Frome, Somerset
Printed and bound in Great Britain by Butler & Tanner Ltd, Frome, Somerset
Colour separation by Dot Gradations, South Woodham Ferrers, Nr Chelmsford
Cover printed by Clays Ltd, St Ives PLC

PICTURE CREDITS

BBC Books would like to thank the following for providing photographs and for permission to reproduce copyright material. While every effort has been made to trace and acknowledge all copyright holders, we would like to apologise should there have been any errors or omissions.
Page 7 Staffordshire Sentinel; 11 Staffordshire Fire & Rescue Service, with special thanks to Station Officer Matthew; 25–31 Press Association; 33 & 36 Mersey Regional Ambulance Service with special thanks to Richard Oswick; 51 & 55 West Midlands Fire Service with special thanks to Divisional Officer Holland; 120–130 Peter de Sousa; 132 Sonat Offshore (UK) Inc; 145 Bristow Helicopters Ltd/Brian Ollington Photographers; 155 *Western Mail & Echo*; 156, 163 & 167 *Lichfield Mercury*; 166 Staffordshire Fire & Rescue Service; 177 Ken Loveday; 190 Crown Copyright/Photographic Section RNAS Culdrose. All other pictures © BBC.
BBC Books would also like to thank Methuen Children's Books for permission to reproduce part of 'The End' from *Now We Are Six* by AA Milne.

CONTENTS

INTRODUCTION

These are stories about heroism, but not necessarily about heroes. For the most part they are accounts of ordinary people who found themselves in extraordinary situations. People who discovered within themselves qualities they never knew existed. At a time of crisis, often at terrible risk, they were able to make the crucial difference that saved lives.

All these stories have been featured in the BBC Television series, 999. From the very first edition, it has proved one of the most popular programmes on the network. The reconstructions of real-life rescues have had a strong appeal to viewers of all kinds. That appeal is based on more than the inherent drama and suspense of each episode. The programme celebrates that which is brave, even noble, about human nature. It shows us that, however much we may have reason to worry about the ills of society, human beings have an immense capacity for selflessness. There is a willingness to help each other to, and beyond, the point of self-sacrifice.

This book, like the television series, is about skill, endurance and, above all, courage. The stories are based on the testimony of those who were there. They have wanted to record the extraordinary events they have witnessed, and pay tribute to the others who were involved.

Each of these events has a lesson for all of us. They are, in a real sense, cautionary tales. Many are extreme illustrations of the dangers implicit in everyday situations – dangers we may avoid, having seen what has happened to others. The most important single lesson, though, is the importance of acquiring a few, basic, first-aid skills. So often in these stories simple skills have saved lives. Many of the stories are followed by concise, easy-to-understand 999 Safety Tips, on how to deal with common emergencies. The idea is that it should be more than a collection of true stories; it is also a manual that could help you save a life, maybe even your own.

MICHAEL BUERK

Beating the Reaper

Afterwards, you realize it was the little things that made the difference between life and death. India Roffey is alive today because more than a dozen people took extraordinary risks to save her; because of the years of training and experience that were called on that night; because the great weight poised to blot out all their lives, did not do so.

But none of that would have made any difference, if there hadn't been mud on the seat.

Sister Kathryn Clayton and
Chief Fire Officer Peter Reid
with 5-year-old India Roffey

India had been listening for the noise of a car, and when the horn beeped that evening, a fortnight before Christmas, she was ready. She was five years old. Her parents had named her after a pop song that had meant a lot to them at the time, but now they were separated. During the week she lived with her mother, Anna, at their house in Alton, Staffordshire. She spent the weekends with her father, Karl, who now lived in a village eight miles down the road.

Anna glanced out of the window, to make sure it was Karl, and India ran down the drive with her overnight things. Anna waved them goodbye and thought no more about it. It was the same every weekend. India would be back tomorrow, in time for school on Monday.

Karl had been fishing that day with his friend, Chris Peters. He was going to drive Chris home after picking up India. When she opened the rear door she saw their fishing gear had made the side she was going to get into muddy, so she went round to the other side. A little thing. But it saved her life.

Jean Gregory and her husband Colin had first spotted the lorry carrying a single, huge container miles back. She had managed to get past it on the dual carriageway coming up towards Doveridge. Then it must have taken a different route, because, as they came up towards the old Crane Marsh Road, there it was again, ahead of them. It was a narrow lane, and a dark wintry night. No chance of overtaking for miles now, she thought.

Karl Roffey's car was coming in the opposite direction. It was a freak accident; to this day nobody has been able to explain properly how it happened. But as Karl's car drew level with the lorry, the container slid sideways, and crushed it under seven and a half tons of metal.

Jean Gregory had fallen some way behind, but saw what had happened when she came round the corner. She braked hard. Colin left the car where it had stopped and ran up the road.

It was only when he got near to the container that he realized there was a car underneath. He ran back to his wife and told her to drive the car up closer and shine the headlights on to the wreckage.

In the headlights, he could see that the massive steel box was lying with one end still on the lorry, the other crushing the driver's side of the car. The car was so crumpled and crushed he was convinced anybody inside would be dead. Jean set off to find a call box and telephone the emergency services.

Colin worked his way round to the passenger side. Through the window, he could see a face. He guessed it might be the driver, who had somehow been forced across the car by the impact. He grabbed the door handle and pulled.

He could only get it to open a crack. As he pulled on it, the man inside seemed to wake up and started shouting. They both heaved and pushed but it would still open only about eight inches. Colin looked at the man inside, who was now kicking at the door in his panic, and thought, He's too big. He'll never get out of a gap this small.

He was wondering what to do next when he noticed that the wrenching and kicking at the door had loosened the glass in the passenger window. Colin got his fingers inside the door frame and managed to pull the glass out in one piece. Then he got hold of the man inside and, big though he was, dragged him out through the window, like toothpaste coming out of a tube.

Chris Peters was not badly injured, but deeply shocked and hysterical. As Colin half carried him to the roadside he kept mumbling about his mate back in the car, and a little girl who was in there too. Colin thought it was hopeless, but promised to go back and look for them.

He went round to the front of the car, and crawled underneath the overhanging container. It was so badly smashed down, he could not imagine any living thing surviving inside. He pushed his hand in through the driver's side window and he could feel a man's body. And it moved.

Karl was coming round. He began screaming with pain and fear. Colin could not see his face because he was crushed down into such a tiny space, jammed hard against the steering wheel. It was obvious he was badly hurt and Colin was sure that his legs were trapped under the steering column.

In between the groaning and shouting Karl managed to get out that his little girl was in the back of the car. Colin reached behind the seat and started to feel around. Down in the floor well, his hand brushed against a tiny, limp arm. Christ, he thought, she's dead.

Under his breath he said, 'She's a gonner.' But he could not tell her father. 'The little girl's fine,' he lied. 'She's all right. She's in the back now. She'll be all right.' At that, Karl seemed to calm down.

But he was obviously in terrible pain, and Colin settled down to wait with him until help arrived.

Once or twice he glanced up at the great steel container, perched precariously above them. If that goes, he thought, I'll be finished too. He tried to ignore it. He concentrated on talking to the driver, trying to get some conviction in his voice when he told him his daughter was fine, they would both be fine.

It was several minutes before he felt able to reach behind the seat again. He found her arm, just as he had before. But this time he felt it give a slight movement.

He called out to her, but there was no reply. Then a tiny hand squeezed his fingers. Colin jumped, so full of emotions his mind did not have time to sort them out. There's some life there, he thought, but God only knows how badly she's injured.

Karl was shouting again with the pain. His screams punctuated a terrible silence. Colin settled down to wait for help to arrive – in that situation every minute felt like for ever.

A single policeman arrived first. Then an ambulance and suddenly, it seemed to Colin, the place was swarming with rescuers. Firemen crawled under the wreckage to where he was still half crouched by the driver's door. He guessed the one in the white helmet was in charge, and asked if he wanted him to get out of the way. But he was told to stay where he was, 'stay with the little 'un, while we try to get the driver out'. In any case, it was obvious the girl did not want to let him go. She would not say anything but clung fiercely to his hand.

The firemen levered at the driver's door with crowbars, but it opened only a little way before it got wedged against the road. They brought up hydraulic equipment and burst the door open, but they still could not get at him properly. The whole of that side of the car had caved in under the tremendous weight of the container. Karl's body was bent round and trapped in the wreckage.

There was no simple solution. It was going to be a long job and, with all that unsecured weight hanging over them, every moment of it was going to be dangerous. They called for more equipment and started to make a plan.

'Why does it always happen at mealtimes?' thought Peter Reid, as he put his phone down. Staffordshire's Chief Fire Officer had had a lifetime of emergencies. A lifetime, his wife Dorothy reminded him, of abandoned meals. Still, he had to go. He enjoyed being the chief, but hated the idea of just dealing with the administration of his service. When all was said and done, he *was* the chief. He was the oldest, which must mean he had the most experience. His place was out there, in charge.

Besides, he had his own, private, reasons for going. The call from fire control had given him only the sketchiest details, but they had said there were children trapped under a massive load. A month before he had been called from his Sunday lunchtime drink to a road crash which had trapped two children in a car. One, thank God, survived. But the other little boy had died from terrible internal injuries. Peter Reid had carried his body to the ambu-

'The whole side of the car had caved in under the tremendous weight of the container'

lance. Seven years old and not a mark on him. He was a sensitive man. Just because you had seen a lot of tragedy did not mean you got used to it. Death had been much on his mind of late and he wanted, more than ever before, to beat it this time. He got in his car and headed for the Crane Marsh Road.

It was a sight he has taken with him into retirement, one that he will remember for the rest of his life. Very dark, very wintry. A great jumble of metal blocking the lane, lit by emergency lights and the blue flashing lights of the rescue vehicles. They had told him it was a crane, but, whatever it was, it certainly was not that. They had told him it probably weighed only four tons, but as he got near it got bigger and bigger, and his practised eye told him it was likely to be double that weight.

At first he could not see how anybody could have survived. The car was crushed right down. Even the uprights of the doors, which normally withstand a lot of pressure, had been telescoped, and the great container seemed to be resting on the top of the driver's seat. Much of the great mass of the container was hanging over the road, 'floating free' as the firemen say. It was obviously unstable, and likely to move at any time. If it did, when it did, anybody underneath would be killed.

Peter Reid was a burly man, but used to working in confined spaces. He pushed himself under the container to make a quick assessment of the casualties. He felt like a mole, burrowing under a huge shed. The great bulk of it took over from the sky. Once you were underneath, there did not seem to be any way out. He started to tot up all the things that could go wrong, but realized it was pointless. He needed a plan, and a prayer.

He called a meeting of the senior firemen, the police, and the medical team – the 'flying squad' that had been called out from the Staffordshire Royal Infirmary. His firemen confirmed his initial impressions of how delicately the weight was balanced. The doctors described Karl Roffey's likely injuries, but could only guess at India's condition. They had only her hand to work on. It was warm. The pulse was strong. But there was no way of telling if she had been hurt, and no way of treating her if she was.

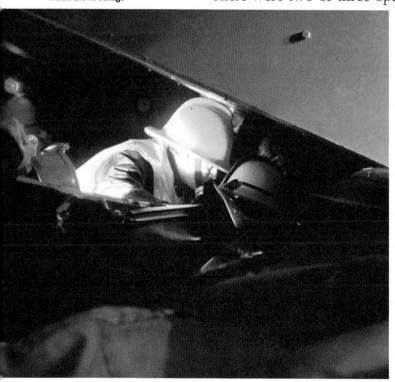

'Peter Reid decided to run the operation from inside the wreckage'

There were two or three options, all of them dangerous. They considered getting a crane in to lift the container straight off the car. The risk would be that the weight would move sideways as the load was taken up. That would almost certainly kill both the people trapped in the car. They decided to leave that as plan B, the last resort.

They decided instead to try to raise the container more slowly from underneath, with air bags and portable power rams placed in five or six positions around it. It would be a complex and delicate operation. The container was lying at an angle. It was unstable, much of it overhanging the car. They would have to move it very slowly, and co-ordinate the lifting points so that it stayed level and did not slip. It would test the firemen's skill to the utmost. And it wasn't just the lives of the casualties that were at stake. Several of their own colleagues would die if they got it wrong.

Including Peter Reid. He decided to run the operation from inside the wreckage. It was the only position where he could assess the whole situation. There he would be able to see what was happening to the car and the casualties, and shout to his men on the lifting gear.

He gave his orders and slipped back underneath the container, taking his helmet off as he went. There just wasn't room to wear it under there – one more danger to worry about.

It was such a small hand. Peter Reid tried to remember what his daughter had been like at that age. He had forgotten how vulnerable they were. He glanced forward at the father and decided he was a straightforward case. He was trapped and sometimes screaming with pain, but they could see him, and could see how they could eventually cut him free. Peter Reid's fire service was responsible for a long stretch of the M6. They did this practically every week; it would just be a matter of time and luck, and the seriousness of his injuries. The girl was different.

In twenty-nine years as a fireman, Peter Reid had never been in a situation where he could see only the casualty's hand. His first impression was how tiny it was, how warm, how eager to clasp his own. There was no simple way to get her out. She was wedged in, down behind the driver's seat, and under the main weight of the container. There would be a lot to shift before they could get to her. It was going to be a long night. Peter Reid tried to visualize his own daughter long ago, and tried to remember what she had liked to talk about.

First, he let her feel his hands and his face, as he told her who he was. It was more than reassurance, he wanted to reinforce the contact she had with her rescuers. He wanted to give her an emotional lifeline to the outside world.

She was calm, even funny. He could not help laughing when she thought his strong Scottish accent was French. She seemed very self-possessed, very much in control.

She told him she was not in pain, but very cramped and crushed. She said she could move her other hand, her feet, and her back. But it was nasty in there, and how long would it be before they got her out?

His instincts were to take it slowly; it would need only a small slip to kill them both. She didn't seem to have injuries that were immediately life-threatening, but he couldn't be sure. Carry on with plan A, and keep talking. There was nothing else he could do.

He talked about his dogs. About the two alsatians, though of course dog lovers like him really called them German Shepherds. How he and Dorothy used to walk labrador puppies for the Guide Dogs for the Blind, and the one called Zara who somehow did not make the grade, and ended up staying with them. He talked about the ducks on his pond. He talked about his favourite colours. He even talked poetry, dredging up from his memory lines he thought somebody her age would appreciate.

When I was One,
I had just begun,
When I was Two,
I was nearly new . . .

It was the ending his daughter had always loved.

Now I am Six, I'm as clever as clever,
So I think I'll be six now for ever and ever.

Just then Peter Reid wanted India to reach six more than anything else in the world.

There were two rescue operations going on simultaneously. Behind the broad back of Peter Reid his firemen were cutting through the bodywork of the car to free Karl Roffey. It was not easy, but it was a job they were trained to do. As long as the container did not move, they knew it was just a matter of time.

But it was not just a cutting operation to get to India. Her life depended on them lifting the container itself. Only then could they move the driver's seat enough to be able to pull her out. That was a much more difficult operation, and more dangerous. The lives of all those working in the wreckage depended on them doing it right. It had to be done very cautiously. It had to be slow.

Too damn slow, thought Peter Reid, as he looked at his watch for the umpteenth time.

Once again he told India not to worry about the noise of the cutting equipment. She really was very composed for such a little girl, but the noise was deafening, and sometimes she thought it was close enough to hurt her.

He was doing his best, but she needed a bit of tender, loving care, above and beyond what a gruff old fireman could provide. Besides, he needed to catch up on what was happening around the wreckage.

He told India he would be back by the time she had counted to ten, and ducked under the wreckage into the wider night.

Sister Kathryn Clayton was waiting by the side of the road. She and two doctors from the North Staffordshire Royal Infirmary formed the flying squad team that stood by to go to the scene of major accidents. So far they had had little to do. There was not much in the way of medical treatment they could provide until the casualties were released.

But it was not strictly medical help Peter Reid was looking for.

It was a mother figure she wanted, he said. Somebody to reassure her and take her mind off what was going on around her. It was dangerous. He knew it, and the sister knew it. But the girl needed her. It was a frightening thing to do, but she said she would.

The tiny hand was still there, poking out of the sleeve of her thick coat. Sister Clayton wondered how injured she might be and how frightened she was behind there. She had so little to go on. Peter Reid introduced her as 'a nice nurse who'd come to say hello'. He held the girl's hand and passed it, first over his face, showing India again how rough it was, then over the sister's smooth one. If only they could see each other's faces, the nurse thought, we would have an idea what she was thinking and how she was coping; some idea of how long we've got to get her out.

It took an hour to free Karl Roffey. He had bad back and leg injuries, but he would live. They were relieved when he had gone. It meant they could concentrate all the effort on the little girl.

A time clock was ticking inside Peter Reid's mind. He couldn't risk speeding up the operation, but he could not let it go on too long. The girl might seem to be all right, but there could be injuries they did not know about, and the delayed effects of shock. They might lose her, and it could happen very quickly. He had seen it so many times before.

Sister Clayton knew she had to stop the girl losing consciousness, and keep her mind off what was going on. The only thing she could think of was to tell her the story of Cinderella. It was working well. Not only was she keeping the girl's attention, but she could get her to respond to points in the story and make sure she was still awake. When she got to the bit about Cinderella going to the ball, for instance, she asked India if she had been to any parties recently. She kept turning the story into a conversation and check.

She spun the story out as long as she could and tried to think of a new one.

To the rescuers who could see them, it was an extraordinary sight. The tiny arm poking out of the mangled wreckage. The nurse on her knees, talking about Cinderella. Peter Reid and another fireman, huddled over her as if they were trying to shield her with their bodies. It was really only a psychological reassurance; they all knew if the container slipped, they would be crushed anyway.

Around them, the firemen working with their air bags and hydraulic rams. Years of experience and training paying off, as they prepared to raise the container.

Then it moved.

Afterwards, they decided it must have been the metal structure of the container adjusting to the different strains as the rams took up the load. But at the time they thought it was starting to slip. The odds of anybody underneath getting out alive had got suddenly worse. Peter Reid took a difficult decision. It was hard enough to justify the danger to his firemen. He could no longer risk a woman's life. He told Sister Clayton she would have to leave.

It was hard for her to tell India she had to go, but you don't question the firemen in circumstances like those. Only a few minutes, she told the little girl. But she wondered if it would be for ever.

When she got outside, she could feel the general sense of tension. An eerie feeling, despite the hiss and clatter of the machinery. The rescue was reaching its climax. The next few minutes would decide whether India, and perhaps some of her rescuers, lived or died.

Peter Reid felt there was not much time left. It was proving a lot more difficult than they had thought. They had lifted the container a little, but still not enough to move the driver's seat. And India, who had been so calm for so long, was showing signs of distress.

It was the noise that was upsetting her. In the confined space

'It was an extraordinary sight. The tiny arm poking out of the mangled wreckage. The nurse on her knees talking about Cinderella'

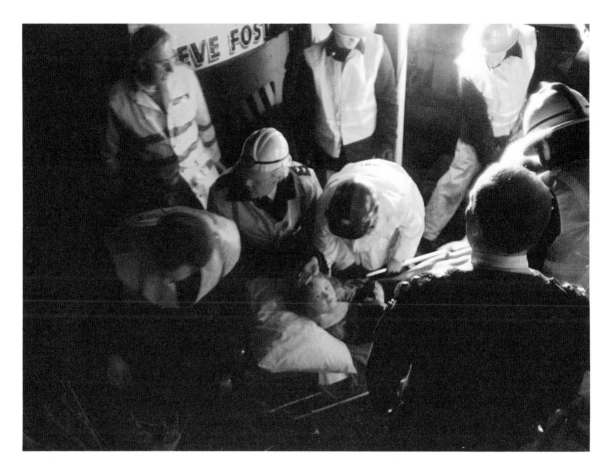

under the wreckage the sound of the firemen's cutting equipment was deafening, and seemed a lot closer to her than it actually was. Peter Reid weighed up the priorities and made a quick decision. He told his men to stop using the compressed-air saw, which was making most of the racket, and use ordinary hacksaws instead. But the girl had already been trapped there for two hours, and that wasn't going to make it any quicker. She kept asking him, 'When am I going to get out of here?' His words were encouraging, but all the time he was thinking, 'I wish to God I knew.'

They cut their way round the seat, replacing the hacksaw blades as they snapped off in their hands. They wrenched at it, but still it wouldn't move. Then Fireman Peter Burton, an ex-Royal Marine, pushed himself right inside the car, across the driver's seat, to try to free it from the other side. It was an extraordinarily dangerous thing to do. But it worked.

'A few seconds later she appeared . . . There was so much tension, so much emotion, even from people who had thought themselves hardened by years of this sort of work'

They felt the seat move, just slightly. A few seconds later – and to this day none of them who was there quite knows how – she appeared, and seemed to propel herself into Peter Reid's arms.

When he carried her out, there was a ripple of cheering from the rescue teams. People were crying. There was so much tension, so much emotion, even from people who had thought themselves hardened by years of this sort of work.

Kathryn Clayton thought the little girl took it like a queen, smiling and waving to her rescuers as she was carried to the ambulance. Inside, the sister checked her over for injuries. There was nothing obvious, except for a small cut on her head. They asked India if she wanted the siren and flashing lights on, which, of course, she did.

The firemen did not seem to want to let her out of their sight. One of the fire engines, loaded down with men, set off in pursuit; others followed. And so, in a convoy of emergency vehicles, India Roffey was carried off to hospital.

They did a thorough check at the accident unit, and confirmed she had escaped serious injury. Sister Clayton was putting a stitch in the cut in her head when India's mother arrived. She hadn't known what to expect, and for several minutes seemed almost paralysed by relief that her daughter was safe and sound. When she started to become aware of her surroundings again, and turned away from India, she was startled to see the room was full of firemen – still kitted up and grimy from working in the wreckage. They had done so much to save her, they still did not want to let her go.

They had a collection for India, and when she came to visit them at the fire station a few days later, they gave her a big teddy bear. She called it Peter Reid, which everybody agreed was entirely appropriate.

Peter Reid, himself, now looks back on that night with pride. Not particularly for his own role, but for the skill and bravery of his men, and the teamwork between all the emergency services.

So many accidents end in tragedy. As he says, it was great on that occasion to beat the reaper.

Sister Kathryn Clayton and Colin Gregory were awarded the Queen's Commendation for Brave Conduct for what they did that night. The bravery of Peter Reid and four of his team was also officially recognized.

Road Accidents – What to do if you're first on the scene

Every year 310,000 people are injured and over 4,000 are killed in traffic accidents in Great Britain. These accidents can be messy and frightening. There may be crashed vehicles, with their crumpled metal and broken glass, as well as people crying in pain from injuries or suffering from shock.

Do the right thing
You may try and avoid getting involved at the scene of an accident simply because it looks so terrifying. But however scared you feel, it's important you do something, especially if you are the first person to arrive at the scene. It's vital to make sure the right kind of help arrives as quickly as possible. And remember that injuries can be made so much worse if would-be rescuers get it wrong. A road accident is different to many other kinds of emergency because the setting itself is potentially dangerous to the rescuer. It is essential to make the area safe – to protect yourself, the casualties and other road users.

Warn others
Many accidents happen at night, on very busy roads and in conditions where bad weather makes it difficult for other drivers to see what has happened well in advance. If you're first on the scene of an accident, park your car at a safe distance (at least 100 yards on a road with a 70 mph limit) behind the crashed vehicles. Switch on your hazard lights and if it's dark leave your headlights on. Try and wear something bright or reflective so you can be seen more easily. If others stop to help, ask them to direct traffic around the accident. Set up warning triangles or lights at least 200 yards in each direction to alert other drivers but ensure that in doing so they don't become a hazard themselves.

Get help
There is little point in the emergency services responding quickly to a 999 call if they have to waste precious time finding the way. It is absolutely crucial to be able to give the location of a road accident as accurately as you can. This may be extremely difficult on a strange country road at night. So whether you are running or driving to the nearest phone, keep an eye out for road signs giving the road number, place names and the approximate distance of the accident to the nearest obvious landmark, such as a pub or church. If you phone from a call box remember it should have its location written on a notice inside. On motorways there are free emergency phones every mile and marker posts with arrows pointing in the direction of the nearest phone every 100 yards. Each marker post also has a number on it which locates your exact position on the motorway; don't forget to give this number when you call for help. There's more detailed information about dialling 999 on page 44.

Ensure your own safety
Always be careful when you approach the scene of an accident and avoid creating further danger. Saving a life may sometimes require an act of heroism, but there is a thin line between heroism and foolhardiness and two casualties are a lot worse than one. It's important to ensure your own safety first. Avoid running across a busy road to try and get

---

Useful things to have in your car for an emergency:

- **FIRST-AID KIT**
- **FIRE EXTINGUISHER**
- **BLANKET**
- **MOBILE PHONE**
- **WARNING TRIANGLE**
- **POWERFUL TORCH**
- **REFLECTIVE JACKET**

REMEMBER
It's an offence not to stop if you're involved in an accident. You are required by law to give your name, address, car registration number and insurance details to the other party. Always make sure you take the names and addresses of any witnesses. If for any reason you are unable to stop you should drive to the nearest police station and report the accident. And if you see people in trouble do stop and help – it could be you who needs that help one day.

help, and never attempt to run across a motorway. Make sure no one smokes – there may be petrol, oil or chemicals spilt on the road. If possible, gather any fire extinguishers in case you need them. The motoring organizations recommend you keep a fire extinguisher in your car and know how and when to use it, but never put yourself in danger when trying to fight a fire.

Hazchem signs

Road traffic accidents may be complicated by the spillage of dangerous chemicals or the escape of toxic fumes. Any vans and lorries carrying such substances must display special 'Hazchem' signs. These signs have flame symbols if they are likely to catch fire spontaneously. They also give a code number and telephone number which you should pass on to the emergency services when you dial 999. Never attempt to rescue anyone from a 'Hazchem' vehicle; it's best to leave it to the

2PE
1230

FLAMMABLE
LIQUID

SPECIALIST ADVICE
(041) 735 35842

professionals, even if there are injured people needing help. Always keep bystanders well away from the scene and remember that any poisonous vapours released can travel some distance. Stand upwind of the accident so that any fumes are blown away from you.

Once you're sure that it's safe to approach the crashed vehicles turn off the ignition key or find the switch marked 'emergency engine cut-off'. Do not move any vehicles involved in the accident until the police arrive and tell you to do so. Stabilize any upright car by applying the handbrake and putting it in gear, but if a vehicle is on its side do not attempt to right it.

Checking the casualties

The most important thing is to assess who needs help first. If you're faced with more than one casualty you must look at each one quickly before making your decision. And remember that appearances may be deceptive. Someone who is shouting or crying is usually less seriously injured than someone who is just moaning. The totally silent person is the one most likely to need help first – their breathing and pulse may have stopped. Check the situation by carrying out the ABC of resuscitation:

AIRWAY
– Open the airway

BREATHING
– Check for breathing

CIRCULATION
– Check the pulse

The *999 Safety Advice* on page 69 illustrates this process in action, and its following first-aid section gives detailed instructions.

It is important that you do not move anyone unless they're in immediate danger. If you are not careful you could risk paralysing them for life. If you have to move anyone, you must have a minimum of five helpers to support their head and neck, keeping them in a straight line with the body. If a motorcyclist is hurt, leave their helmet on because of the risk of neck injury. Only remove it as a last resort, if they aren't breathing or they're vomiting. Always stay at the scene of an accident until help arrives. Try and reassure the casualties and keep them warm.

'It was a colossal explosion. The blast tore the heart out of the building and left a gap fifty yards wide, framed by ruins'

CHAPTER 2

Big Bang

The moment they woke up they smelt it. Everybody in that block of flats remembers the strong, almost sweet, smell of gas that morning. Everybody who survived, that is.

Eva and Karen Krejci lived at number 9. They had been born in Czechoslovakia, but now the sisters shared a flat together on the first floor of Newnham House, one of the 1930s blocks that make up the Manorfields estate in Putney, south-west London. It was a pleasant place to live, well-kept and set back from the main road that climbs away from the river towards the suburban sprawl of south London and the soft countryside of Surrey beyond.

The sisters were still asleep when the estate caretaker started work. Normally, Garrit 'Dutchy' Gellisen liked being up and about before everybody else. That morning he wished he had a job where he could stay in bed. It was going to be another bitter January day. That week the temperature had dropped to −5°C. The wind cut you open like a razor and it was snowing hard.

Still, 'Dutchy' was there at six as usual, emptying the bins. He took the milk over to the estate office, and sorted out the mail for the flats. There was a parcel for Karen Krejci but he decided to wait a while before delivering it. There would be complaints if he went round knocking on people's doors before seven.

Eva and Karen got up at quarter to seven to have breakfast together before going to work. The smell of gas was everywhere and it seemed to Eva, as she made the coffee, it was getting stronger all the time. They talked about what they should do, and Eva promised to ring the Gas Board as soon as she got to work.

Their neighbours had already done so. Michael Ashcroft and his wife in number 12 had known straightaway there was something wrong. The records show she phoned the South Eastern Gas Board at two minutes past seven. He went round the other flats to warn them about the gas and tell them it had been reported. He knocked on the sisters' door and spoke to Karen. He wanted to stop anybody lighting matches or setting off a spark until the smell had been investigated.

'Dutchy' Gellisen smelt the gas as soon as he came into the building. He spoke to both the Krejci sisters about it when he handed over the parcel. They urged him to phone the Gas Board as well. He said he would as soon as he got back to the estate office. On his way out he threw open all the windows in the stairwell. But the smell was still there.

Eva Krejci went into the bathroom and started to run her morning bath. She turned to clean her teeth. Outside, 'Dutchy' Gellisen had crossed the courtyard and was just putting his key in the door of the estate office, wondering where he would find the Gas Board's emergency number.

It was fourteen minutes past seven when their world was blown to pieces.

It was a colossal explosion. It was heard across much of London and for some time thought to be an IRA bomb. The centre section of the block of flats collapsed into a great pile of rubble and dust. The blast tore the heart out of the building and left a gap fifty yards wide, framed by ruins.

'Dutchy' Gellisen felt, rather than heard, a great bang and was lifted right off his feet. A paper boy just going into one of the other blocks saw a blinding flash and was hurled into a wall. The explosion blew the doors off an old people's home across the street, and shattered windows half a mile away. Up the road, the landlord of the Green Man on Putney Hill woke up to see his bedroom windows being sucked out, along with a glass that had been on the windowsill. He thought his new boiler had blown up and was surprised to find the pub was more or less intact. Outside, he saw a policeman running up the hill with his helmet missing, holding a notebook. The policeman asked him what had happened, but by then he did not need to tell him. One glance over his left shoulder at what was left of Newnham House was enough.

'It was fourteen minutes past seven when their world was blown to pieces'

The London Fire Brigade's headquarters is a big old building on the Albert Embankment that runs along the south bank of the Thames. By contrast, the control room at its heart is all late twentieth-century, air-conditioned efficiency. Men and women in shirtsleeves sit at their consoles and deal with more than 500 calls a day, calming the callers, assessing, and distributing, the appeals for help. The long wall at one end of the room is covered with a map of greater London. It shows the capital's 113 fire stations, the number of fire appliances available, and the state of readiness of the crews. On the left-hand side of the wall, the emergencies they are dealing with are listed on a scrolling, electronic display, like the departure board at an airport. At any moment, the wall gives you a snapshot of a great city's misfortunes and how it is coping with them.

The first calls about the Putney explosion came in three minutes after it had happened, but word had already started to get around. They couldn't hear it in the control room, but staff who had been out in the car park or the street said they had heard it, even though it was four miles away. Most assumed it was a bomb.

In the minutes that followed, the consoles lit up and clicked as call after call came through. It was a major incident and the fire brigade responded accordingly. Nearly sixty firefighters were sent, but there was no fire to fight and, after the first few minutes, it did not look as though there was anybody left alive to rescue.

Within half an hour of the first call, the firemen had established it was a gas explosion, not a bomb. They had reported back to headquarters that forty-five per cent of the building – a remarkably precise estimate – had been destroyed, and that sixteen people were thought to be missing.

By eight o'clock, they had freed four people who had been trapped on the second floor. They were the Ashcrofts, who had reported the gas leak an hour before. They lived at the side of the building and their flat had escaped the main force of the explosion. It was relatively intact, but the staircase had been destroyed and they had been unable to get out.

The firemen started to recover bodies, some so mutilated by the force of the blast as to be almost unrecognizable. It was already clear, though, that the operation was going to be a long and dangerous one. They had to use their bare hands because they were afraid their mechanical equipment would bring down the rest of the building: one of the first calls back to headquarters was for more shovels. They imposed an immediate radio blackout in the area because they thought there was a real danger that static electricity might set off a second explosion. The only electronic equipment they allowed on the site was their new thermal imaging cameras to try to detect the heat of a human body under the cold rubble.

Not that any of the firemen expected to find survivors. Peter Simpson had taken one look when he had arrived, and resigned himself to a long and depressing search for the dead. He had never seen devastation like it. The whole centre section of the three-storey block had been reduced to a pile of debris. He was sure nobody inside any of those flats could have survived.

The set procedure for major emergencies in that part of London nominates Queen Mary's Hospital as the main centre for the treatment of casualties. It had been alerted in the minutes following the explosion and off-duty doctors and nurses were called in to help man the accident and emergency unit, for what was expected to be a flood of injured people.

One of those bleeped was Barry Powell, a plastic surgeon and senior registrar, who had been on duty the previous night. As they gathered in the accident unit, another call came through for a medical team to go to the scene of the explosion. He volunteered, arguing strongly that his training and his background in trauma medicine and emergency first aid would be useful on site. It would allow the specialist accident and emergency staff to stay in the casualty unit, where it was still thought they would be most needed. He climbed into a police car along with a consultant surgeon. Sirens blaring, blue lights flashing, they headed for Putney.

In another police car not far behind, Rona MacKay was feeling frightened. She was a casualty sister at Queen Mary's, and had been off-duty in the nurses' home when the call came through. It had all happened so fast. Now she was sitting next to an anaesthetist, with an amputation set on the seat between them. Neither knew what to expect and both were worried about what they would find.

The medical team got there at a quarter past eight. Most of south London seemed in chaos because of the explosion, and there was pandemonium around that part of Putney, with traffic gridlocked and tempers short. The damage was much worse than any of them had expected, even after hearing early reports on the radio.

Once the scale of the whole thing had sunk in, what struck Rona MacKay was the sound of telephones ringing from under the wreckage. She realized it must be the friends and relatives of the people who lived in those flats, ringing up to see if they were all right; phones nobody would ever answer. A few minutes later they all stopped at once. She assumed British Telecom had cut the lines.

There was little for them to do. Barry Powell was called away twice by the city coroner's officer to examine the bodies of people found in the rubble and certify them dead. Given the nature of their injuries, it was only a formality.

For the most part they stood around in the biting cold.

Dr Barry Powell, a plastic surgeon and senior registrar at Queen Mary's Hospital in London at the time of the explosion

Somebody went to find Rona some gloves and came back with a long, black, evening pair. She pushed the phials of intravenous fluid down the front of her bra to keep them from freezing, and wondered how long it would be before they gave up and she could go back to the hospital.

The fire crews were well aware of the dangers they ran as they looked for the bodies. Much of the block that was still standing was unstable, and picking their way through the rubble by hand carried a constant threat of being buried under the debris if it moved. The main worry was a huge chunk of masonry, jutting out at roof level from what was left of the building, and hanging over part of the site where the firemen were working. It could fall at any time and, if it did, could well kill several of the rescuers. For their safety, they should have brought it down, but they did not want to do that if there was the slightest chance of finding somebody alive. Instead, they posted a man under it with a whistle, and hoped he would have time to warn them if it moved.

By eleven o'clock what little hope there had been had run out. They had been working for nearly four hours and uncovered nothing but dead bodies. Many felt it was time to pull the overhang down, to speed up the clearance operation. The medical team, frozen stiff and despondent, gathered their equipment to return to the hospital.

The firemen made a last effort. They whistled and called out; they banged bricks and tapped on bits of the wreckage. One of them thought he heard a reply. There was a tapping noise, he said, coming from under the rubble.

The word spread round in seconds. The loudspeakers called for quiet. Everybody stopped work, the noise dropped away and a ghostly silence fell over the site. The tension held them all.

They knocked out another signal, and this time they were sure. Several of them heard the tapping. Somebody was alive under there.

The thermal imaging cameras were brought over to try to fix the casualty's position. The crews of the emergency tenders, men experienced at lifting and cutting through wreckage, were given the job of finding him, or her. They split up into two teams. One went round the back of the building, made its way through a staircase shaft and then started digging through the rubble from there. The second team tried to get through from the other side, through a broken roof section.

They had to claw their way through the wreckage inch by inch, brick by brick, trying at the same time to make sure it did not collapse on top of them. The work was agonizingly slow, and the further they tunnelled into the debris, the more dangerous it became. But the mood had changed now. It was no longer a desolate search for the dead. There was a life to be saved. A new sense of urgency and purpose drove them on.

It was half an hour later that one of the firemen came across to Barry Powell and told him they had found a human foot. They did not know if it was a man or a woman, alive or dead. He led him round to the back of a pile of rubble, and they clambered halfway up it, to the point where the firemen had been digging. They had found the foot nearly a yard into the debris. When he peered down at a forty-five-degree angle into the hole, he could see it was still wearing a slipper. He examined it as best he could. It was a woman's foot, he could tell that much, but it was cold, and did not move. There was no way of telling if the woman was still alive, and it was impossible to say for sure if she had been the source of the tapping. What he could see was that the leg had been crushed by a block of masonry, which effectively prevented them getting any nearer to her from that angle. The first team was still digging from the other side; the second looked for a new place to start a fresh tunnel.

Eva was drifting in and out of consciousness and had been ever since she first came to, wondering if she was alive, or dead and this was her tomb. She remembered the moment of the blast, being lifted into the air and everything going black. In that split-second she knew the gas had blown up. Then that thought, and everything else, was sucked away into oblivion.

'The word spread round in seconds. The loudspeakers called for quiet. Everybody stopped work, the noise dropped away and a ghostly silence fell over the site'

When she woke, she was on her side in the dark, bent almost double in a pool of water. She felt no pain but did not know that was because her back was broken as well as her legs. It was the cast iron bath that had saved her. A great chunk of masonry from the roof was lying across it, and the upper part of her body was in a small gap underneath.

She was convinced she was going to die, and was resigned to it. It was a shame to go at thirty-five, she thought, but it had been a good life. At one point she heard helicopters passing overhead and wondered what they were doing. It did not occur to her that they were the photographers from the newspapers and television companies filming what was left of her home. She was not to know that she was already listed among the victims of the worst gas explosion for decades.

Some time later she sensed movement in the rubble around her, and heard firemen talking somewhere over her head. The only thing she could move was her left hand. She felt around until she found a piece of brick, and began hitting the bathroom lino where she was lying. That was what they heard on the surface; the tapping that stopped them burying her even deeper.

It was all taking a long time. There was so much rubble to move, and it was so unstable it was impossible to shore up the tunnels properly. The further they drove into the wreckage, the greater the danger the whole thing would collapse. There was no shortage of back-up; chains of firemen carried the debris away, brick by brick. But it was all down to their courage and skill; pulling the rubble out bit by bit, chipping away, propping up, and testing over and over to see if the hole they were making would let them through or kill them. It was, as one of them said, trial and error – with no room for error.

After two hours' digging, they were asked if they wanted to be relieved by other crews, but they refused. Only they knew the complexity and the dangers of their tunnels. Besides, from time to time, they could hear her moaning. They each now felt a personal commitment to getting her out, and would not give up.

It was well past one o'clock before they got to what was left of the Krejcis' bathroom. Eva had been trapped for more than five hours. The team trying to reach her from the back of the building

'She was convinced she was going to die, and was resigned to it. It was a shame to go at thirty-five, she thought, but it had been a good life'

got as far as locating where she was, but found they could not reach her from that side and had to go back. The other team pressed on. It was now all up to them.

Peter Simpson was the first fireman to get close enough to Eva to talk to her. It was gone half-past one when he was able to get her to respond to what he was saying, while they tried to punch through the wall of rubble to get through to her. She was crying a little, but mostly calm. At that time she thought she was the only casualty, and kept asking about her sister. He told her everything was being done, which was true, as well as being the standard reply to questions that could not be answered.

Fifteen minutes later, they had opened a small hole and could see her at last, crouched in a small space and crushed up against the bath. She was wearing a towelling robe and was tangled up in the plastic clothes rails that had been hanging in the bathroom.

After they had widened the hole and secured the loose flooring, they were able to push themselves full length into the space, close enough now to reach out and touch her.

They asked her her name, and how she felt. She was rational and able to reply, but told them she could feel nothing. The firemen were close enough now to see how badly her legs were crushed. They tried to reassure her, to tell her she would soon be out of there, though they knew it was not going to be as simple as that. They held her hand and made every effort they could to keep her talking, but she kept drifting away.

She must still have been half-conscious because she has a clear memory of a fireman saying they should amputate her leg to free her. 'We might as well,' she heard him say, 'because it won't be any use to her any more.' She remembers being frightened, and hoping she would have a say in whether her leg came off or not, but then she must have lost consciousness completely.

Once they had reached her, the firemen urgently needed to know how serious her injuries really were, and how much time they had left. They called Barry Powell and asked if he would go down to assess whether she would survive long enough to let them get her out carefully, or whether her life depended on pulling her out immediately, as best they could.

Only one person could work in the tunnel at a time, so they had to come out to let him in. He was not a man suited to working in confined spaces. He had never liked the feeling of being hemmed in and, besides, he was a huge man, 6ft 4in tall and weighing 17 stone. He was able to get into the entrance on his hands and knees, but then the tunnel narrowed at an acute angle and he had to push his way through on his stomach. He had to crawl nearly ten feet, right into the wreckage, to get near her. His knees and elbows were cut by broken bricks and all the time he was aware that there were tons of debris on top of him; one wrong movement could bring it all down on top of him. Somehow he was able to suppress his fear. He was being driven by adrenalin and buoyed up by the competence, and confidence, of the firemen: the shared purpose of saving the woman's life.

To start with, he could not see her properly, but the firemen widened the space so that he could reach in and touch her arm. Her hand felt warm, and there was a good pulse. He asked her if she could wiggle her toes, but she said she could not feel anything below her waist. Before he could examine her further, the firemen pulled him out because they were worried the tunnel would collapse and they wanted to do more work to shore it up.

A few minutes later he went back in, and this time he was able to take a closer look at her injuries. The worst thing he could see was the damage to her knee. It had been smashed by falling rubble, and the leg was almost severed. Again, though, the firemen ordered him out, this time because they were afraid the overhanging masonry was going to fall.

When they let him back in a third time he took a drip with him, a plasma expander that could feed in painkillers as well as blood. The sister had prepared it, and normally inserting it would be a nurse's job. He was a bit out of practice, and the conditions were hardly what anybody would call ideal. He felt some pride when he was able to get it in the vein first time.

In the end he decided she did not need painkillers. The nerve damage had stopped the injuries hurting too much. And the piercing cold had helped constrict her blood vessels, preventing too much bleeding. What she needed was to get out of there and into hospital, and his professional instinct told him that time was running out, and they had to take some tough decisions.

She was lying with her head furthest away from the tunnel and the people trying to rescue her. There was no room to turn her

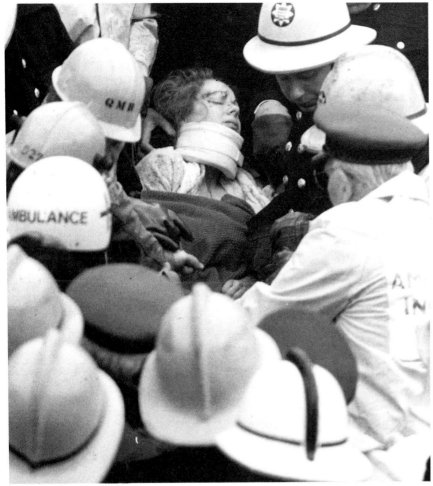

'She was conscious when they brought her out . . . It was, she thought, like being born again . . . the most wonderful experience of her life'

round to drag her out by the arms and they were worried that if they tried to make the space bigger it would all come down on top of them. In any case there was too little time.

The only option was to drag her out by the legs, even though the right one was so badly damaged she might lose it as they pulled her through the tunnel. They discussed amputating it there and then, but decided there might still be chance of saving it. Besides, amputation would also mean a dangerous delay.

The last fifteen minutes were the most difficult and frustrating for the fire crews, clearing away the piping and other debris that were still in the way. Nerve-racking, too, for Barry Powell, who had returned and was now waiting at the entrance to the tunnel with a cervical collar to put on Eva to protect her broken back.

It was gone two o'clock when they decided to try to move her. They were worried about how they would get her round a jack they had had to place near her legs to hold the roof up. And they could only get a real purchase on the badly injured right leg, but they could wait no longer. As gently as they could, they pulled her across the floor of what looked like – and should have been – her tomb, and into the tunnel. As soon as they had moved her a little way one of the firemen was able to tie her legs together with his scarf, making one a splint for the other. Then they pushed and pulled her up towards the daylight.

She was conscious when they brought her out, after seven hours in the ruins. It was, she thought, like being born again. The daylight was the best thing she had ever seen. The feel of the fresh air, the sight of the wide sky, the most wonderful experiences of her life.

They put her on a stretcher and passed her along a line of firemen to the waiting ambulance.

Eva survived, but nine people, including her sister Karen, died in the explosion. Eva was in hospital for seven months and had more than forty operations. A thousand people sent her get-well cards, including the former cabinet minister, Norman Tebbit, who was badly injured, and his wife crippled, by the IRA bomb that blew up the Grand Hotel in Brighton.

Eva's recovery was slow, but eventually she was able to walk again. Her greatest support during that long convalescence was a man who was no more than an acquaintance at the time of the accident. Richard Olsen heard the news of the explosion on his car radio that morning as he drove to Heathrow to catch a flight to the United States. He had some premonition Eva was involved and drove to Putney instead. It was not until that evening that he knew for certain she had been rescued, and he was told then she probably would not walk again. He visited her regularly in hospital and promised to take her to Ascot races if she was well enough. It gave her something to work for, and him quite a problem. By the time they realized she would be fit enough to go, all the passes for the members' enclosure had gone. He wrote to Buckingham Palace, explaining the situation, and one of the Queen's staff sent them two special tickets.

Eva is now Mrs Richard Olsen.

CHAPTER 3

The Miracle Man

Mark Hayes was walking across a field in the dark. He didn't know where he was going, just getting away, looking for somewhere to rest. He can remember thinking of his wife and his baby. Who was going to tell them that he had gone?

That seems to be what made him turn round and go back. He stood by the fence, and could see it all. The wrecked lorry, the fire engines and ambulances. People everywhere, working under the emergency lights. He could see one of the firemen holding a wooden stake that had punched straight through the cab of the lorry, and through the man inside. And the man was him.

He screamed because the pain had come back. But it was the moment he decided to live.

Mark Hayes smiling as he stands in front of the reconstructed accident

Scientists can explain how the body works, how injury or disease can damage it, and tell you afterwards why a man died. But all the medical research of the twentieth century cannot explain what links us to life. It is spiritual, as well as physical. How else do you explain how one man may die, yet another with far worse injuries survives?

How else do you explain why Mark Hayes is still alive?

Mark often got a lift home in one of the firm's lorries. It was not far, half an hour or so down the M53, to the flat where he lived with his wife and baby daughter. He was keen to get home that May evening. He and Sue had known each other since they were sixteen, and had gone out together for eight years before they had got married the year before. Little Ashley was only seven weeks old. She had been more than a month premature, so when you worked it out you could say she was really only a fortnight old. They were both totally absorbed by her. Ashley had changed their lives.

It happened suddenly, and for no apparent reason. The lorry went out of control and it veered across the hard shoulder and down an embankment towards a wooden fence. If he had kept going they would have gone straight through the fence, into a field and both of them would probably have been able to walk away. But he tried to wrench it back towards the road, and hit the fence end-on.

The lorry careered along the line of the fence, demolishing fifty yards of it. Two of the horizontal poles smashed into the cab. One went through Mark's chest just below the breast bone. The other went into his groin, out through the left side of his back, through the seat he was sitting on, and three or four feet into the engine compartment behind the cab. That should have been the end of the story; the end of him. But it was not.

He had felt the lorry tip down the embankment. He had heard the wood snapping and cracking – then the windscreen smash. When the lorry stopped he felt numb. He opened his eyes and saw the poles sticking into him and screamed as he felt the pain for the first time. Then all the feeling went away again.

His eyelids felt heavy. But, somewhere inside him, he could hear a voice saying, 'If you let your eyes shut you'll die, and you'll lose your little girl.'

Dave Owen and Andy Hartley were on standby that night, parked

'All the medical research of the twentieth century cannot explain what links us to life. It is spiritual as well as physical'

up in their ambulance on a garage forecourt halfway between Ellesmere Port and Chester, talking about cars. Cars had been on Dave's mind a lot that day. He had just bought a new one, and was rapidly coming to the conclusion that the old one was better. 'Too late now,' he said, not for the first time.

Mark was lucky that night. Dave and Andy were only six miles away from where he had crashed. As far as the Chester Ambulance Service was concerned, Dave was unique. He had been an ambulanceman for fifteen years, but only six weeks earlier he had qualified as a paramedic. At that time he was Chester's only paramedic, and he was there at the crash four minutes after taking the call, made by a motorist who had witnessed the accident.

The lorry did not look too badly damaged, but the driver was standing in front of it holding on to a piece of wood and yelling at them, 'For God's sake hurry, he's in a bad way.' Dave left Andy to park the ambulance and ran over to the cab, carrying his paramedic's emergency box and a blanket. When he got close he could see the casualty, half lying, half sitting, between the seats.

He was dead. Or if he wasn't dead now he soon would be. Dave was usually right about things like that. He could tell when a casualty was going to make it, and nobody could survive those kinds of injury. He was surprised when Mark opened his eyes.

He almost fell over when he spoke.

Mark asked the question he was to ask over and over again, as long as he stayed conscious: 'Am I going to die?' Dave cannot remember what he said, only what he thought: 'To be perfectly honest, yes, you are.'

He brushed the glass off the seat and knelt on it, cradling Mark's head in his lap. He had to take his weight because he could not move him; he was being held in place by one of the poles, which had effectively skewered him to the seat. It had done terrible damage to his lower abdomen, carrying away some of his insides, which were still wrapped around the wood that had impaled him. The second pole had smashed his left lung, and there were no chest sounds on the left-hand side. His breathing was very shallow. He was obviously in extreme shock. His pulse rate was very weak and rapid; the blood pressure was low. Dave thought he must have lost more than five pints of blood. He ought to be looking at a dead man, but Mark would not die.

Dave did what he could. He cut Mark's clothes away from around

'Dave Owen's main concern was to get some fluid into Mark's body to replace all the blood he had lost'

the poles, and wadded the wounds around the wood to try to reduce the bleeding.

Mark felt himself drifting. He must have passed out for a while because, when he woke up, someone was asking him what his name was. How old was he? Was he married? Had he got any children? Talking was terribly difficult, he was gasping for every breath. But he told the paramedic about Sue and Ashley. He wondered how they would get to hear about the accident. After a while his eyes began to feel heavy again. His head swam and he thought he was going to be sick.

Dave Owen tried hard to keep him talking. It was the best way of monitoring his condition, the only hope of keeping him alive.

Help arrived within minutes. First, the motorway police, then two fire engines and the rescue tender. Firemen came running from all directions. One took over from the lorry driver the vital job of supporting the lower pole. Others came up to the cab to help.

Dave's main concern was to get some fluid into Mark's body to replace all the blood he had lost. He got one of the firemen to hold Mark's arm while he attached a drip; his hands were shaking so much he was afraid he would miss the vein. Soon, though, he had a fireman each side, both holding drips. He just gave them the bag and said, 'Here, take this. Squeeze it occasionally and for God's sake give me a shout when it's nearly empty.'

Dave found it difficult to understand how Mark stood the pain. He was obviously a strong lad, but the slightest movement made him scream. Dave wondered how he himself would cope. Dead long ago, he thought, and maybe grateful for it.

Fireman Geoff Roberts thought most people would have let themselves die. In twenty years in the fire service he had seen some terrible injuries, but nothing like this. Since he had arrived he had been helping to keep Mark talking. He was standing on the front bumper, no more than a couple of feet away, watching the life in him ebb and flow. Every so often Mark would drift away and the two of them would have to shout at him to wake him up. They found the best thing was to mention his wife and baby. It was magic, really, the way the fight in him would rise up when they mentioned their names.

By now, the flying squad from the Countess of Chester Hospital had arrived and the doctor had given Mark some painkillers. But there was no room for him to work, and little more he could do anyway. Dave had already given him fluids and oxygen, and dressed his wounds as well as he could in the conditions. He took Mark's heart, pulse, blood pressure and respiration readings at periodic intervals because the training courses he had just been on said the information was vital when the casualty got back to the operating theatre. Normally he would have written it all down in a notebook. But it was so cramped, and he was so tense, he wrote the figures on his hand. Soon he had to carry on up his arm, and eventually had to write some of it down on a fireman's hand when he had totally run out of space.

He had done everything he could for Mark. Now it depended on how fast the firemen could get him out, and whether Mark could hold on.

Geoff Roberts knew a thing or two about getting people alive out of wrecked vehicles, and he did not think they would manage it this time. The lower pole pinned Mark into place, with several feet either side of him wedged into the wreckage. The other pole stuck five or six feet out of his chest. He was connected to at least two drips, and an electrocardiograph machine that was monitoring his heart – all of which had to stay in place if he was to stay alive.

Geoff thought his chances had been slim when he first saw him; now he thought they were as close to nil as made no difference.

The firemen decided they would have to lift him out, and began cutting at the roof of the cab to give themselves more room. Mark drifted back to consciousness at that point and knew exactly what they were doing. A few months before he had done a fire service course. He had not, in the end, become a fireman, but he had been taught how to cut through a crashed vehicle and recognized the sound of the hydraulic saw. Then he lost consciousness again, and felt his spirit leave his body.

It was an out-of-body experience he can still remember vividly. Leaving his body behind and walking away across the fields, towards the border between life and death. The thought of his wife and child that seemed to stop him at the last moment and make him return. The very point at which he should have died, but chose not to do so.

For his rescuers, the most difficult part of the operation was clearly going to be cutting the poles that still transfixed Mark and pinned him into the wreckage. A hacksaw would jar the wood, and make it turn – almost certainly enough to kill him. The firemen practised with a piece of broken wood, and decided a compressed-air saw was likely to do the least damage.

Dave Owen told them to go ahead, but carefully. 'If I shout stop, just bloody stop.' Mark was conscious as they cut into the first pole, about four inches from his body, but not for long. He gave a last scream, and passed out. Dave Owen checked his blood pressure and his heartbeat. Both were deteriorating. He pumped in more painkillers and told them to carry on. There was not going to be much time.

The lower pole proved to be the main problem. It was embedded in the seat so they had to cut the upholstery away, and then cut each spring individually with a pair of pliers. When they had finished he was free. But they still had to lift him out.

His injuries were so severe there was no question of immobilizing him. They did not know if he had spinal injuries, so when they started to move him they ran the risk of paralysing him for life. Yet, somehow, they had to lift him over the dashboard and the steering wheel, down over the front of the cab and out to the waiting ambulance. They knew the slightest movement could aggravate his internal injuries, maybe reopen the damaged arteries. And the stakes were still in him; just touching one of the cut ends against the bodywork could be enough to kill him. No wonder Geoff Roberts and the other firemen did not think it could be done.

It was close to a miracle, but they did it. Six people lifted him off the seat, inch by inch and passed him over the dashboard. Another six took him over the front of the lorry and put him in the most comfortable position they could on the stretcher.

All the time Dave Owen had been on his knees, taking Mark's weight. His own legs were paralysed with cramp and he had to be helped into the ambulance so he could continue to look after him.

The firemen's job was finished at last. Most traffic accident rescues are over in fifteen minutes, but this one had been such a

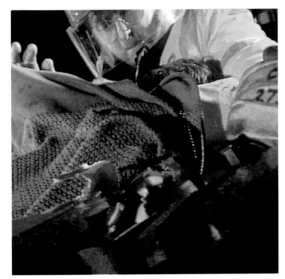

delicate operation it had taken well over an hour. They were euphoric, but realistic. Geoff Roberts says they still didn't expect him to survive. They didn't even think he would make it to the hospital.

A few miles away Sue Hayes was more angry than worried as the minutes ticked away, rehearsing the telling-off she was going to give Mark when he finally came home. The rational part of her had long ago decided Mark must have stopped off at the pub with his mates. But there was something irrational nagging away at the back of her mind which time, and subsequent events, have made her think it was some kind of premonition. Something about the way he had kissed them both and lingered with them before he went off to work, when normally he would have shot out of the door in his usual early-morning panic. Something, too, about the way Ashley had cried so bitterly long after he had gone. It all seems significant to her now.

Even so, when there was a knock on the door at a quarter to eleven that night she thought Mark had lost his keys. She was not expecting the police.

Dave Owen was prepared for Mark to die at any moment. He had done all the checks again. He had connected the oxygen lines and the ECG monitors, he had checked for a femoral pulse, to see if the

999 (Left) 'The firemen decided they would have to lift him out, and began cutting at the roof of the cab'
(Above) 'His injuries were so severe . . . when they started to move him they ran the risk of paralysing him for life'

blood was still flowing to his legs. He had told the driver to go slowly. One lurch, he had told him, could be enough to kill him. The police cars cleared the way, as Mark headed for the Countess of Chester Hospital, with the man who had stopped him dying standing anxiously over him.

The man who would give him his life back was waiting in the accident and emergency unit. James Kane had been on call at home when the ambulance contacted the hospital to tell them about the case they were bringing in. The duty registrar told the surgeon over the phone that the man was badly hurt, but he was not prepared for what he saw that night. He had never come across such severe injuries. His first thought was that the two thick slabs of wood still in him must have caused enormous internal injuries. His second was to wonder how he had stayed alive so long. The third, that his chances of surviving much longer were extremely remote. It wasn't an encouraging start.

In resuscitation they tried to make sure he could breathe and hooked him up to new fluid and blood drips. They put drains into both sides of his chest. At the end of it, he was still alive.

They took him to the operating theatre. Mr Kane found it difficult to know where to start. Mark's ribs were broken, his lung was punctured, his diaphragm was ruptured, his spleen and his pancreas were finished, and both his small and large bowel were badly damaged. His heart was untouched – one pole has passed within an inch of it – and the poles had somehow missed the main arteries, but almost everything else, from his collar bone to his groin, was smashed. The surgeon looked at the wreckage of Mark's groin and thought even if he lived he would never be able to father another child. At the time, though, that seemed a minor consideration.

That first operation took nearly seven hours. The poles were removed, but they had spread splinters through the lower part of Mark's body and had driven scraps of material from his shirt and jeans into his abdominal cavity. Many of the damaged organs had to be removed.

A piece of wood, four inches by two inches, four feet long, pushed right through the body, does a lot of destruction. Both pieces left enormous wounds.

At the end of that first long night of surgery he was still alive, but only just.

'Dave Owen was prepared for Mark to die at any moment'

Having left baby Ashley with her mother, Sue had arrived at the hospital just before he had been taken into the operating theatre but they would not let her see him. She sat there all night, numb with all that had happened, drinking the tea they kept bringing.

It was dawn when a woman doctor came to see her. She told Sue what had happened to her husband, but she couldn't take it in. She did not want to hear. It was too much to cope with all at once.

The doctor said they had done all they could. She told her, 'Mark is in God's hands now.' That is all she can remember.

They took her in to see him in intensive care an hour later. He was wired up with tubes in his nose and his arms. She could not see his injuries because most of his body was covered in foil to keep him warm during the long hours on the operating table. Even so, when she touched him he felt stone cold. She broke down then and, for a second, he appeared to acknowledge her. He blinked and she thought he was trying to speak. The nurses ran over and gave him more drugs and he slipped off into unconsciousness.

The doctors told her he was stable, but might go at any time. She realizes now they were preparing her for his death. One told her it would be a miracle if he survived the next six hours.

Someone took her to her mother's house and she collapsed. She woke up a few hours later convinced that she was a widow. But when she rang the hospital he was still alive.

Mark was on a respirator in the intensive care ward. He survived that day, and the next. But on the third day after the accident he started to deteriorate. The medical team had been half expecting it and took him back into the operating theatre. They found that fragments of wood and clothing left inside him had set up an infection. They were difficult to spot, and each time the surgeons looked they found more. It was obvious they were going to have to open him up several times to deal with recurrent infections so they fitted him with a surgical zip – just like the zip in a windcheater – across his stomach to avoid having to make a new incision each time. In the weeks that followed they did eight more operations to wash infection out of his abdominal cavity before they felt it was safe to remove the zip and let the wound heal.

Sue had been given a room in the hospital and she stayed there for the next three and a half weeks. At first it had been hour to hour, then day to day; each a hurdle to get over, a triumph over death.

But no one victory would guarantee the next. To start with, Sue spent most of her time crying but, little by little, she began to help care for him. She washed and shaved him. She put ice packs on him to cool him down, even changed the dressings on his terrible wounds.

After the first fortnight, the fear that he might die was replaced by worry over what sort of life he would have if he survived. There was the possibility of brain damage, of paralysis. He had been a fit young man before the accident, and a fine footballer. A loving husband, always fun to be with. What sort of person would he be after all the trauma he had gone through and the drugs they had used?

After three weeks they began slowly to reduce the morphine they were giving him to control the pain, to wean him away from dependence. It made him restless and he would try to pull the tubes out of his body. On the whole, they considered that a good sign.

June was almost over when Mark regained consciousness. The last thing he could remember was the vivid flash of pain when the fireman had been cutting through the pole, and the paramedic shouting, 'Stop!' The next thing he knew he was in intensive care with the doctors, half hidden behind a sheet, examining his stomach. Mr Kane leaned over and asked him what day it was.

Mark thought back. The accident had been on a Monday, so it must be Tuesday.

'I don't think so,' the surgeon said. 'Try six weeks later. Welcome back.'

The next few weeks were painful and disturbing for Mark as the doctors continued to reduce the doses of morphine. He had to suffer the withdrawal symptoms that drug addicts face, hallucinations and the sudden sweating the clinics call 'cold turkey'. On top of that he had to find new ways of coping with the pain.

It was a difficult time for Sue. At first it was a huge relief when they were able to talk, and he told her what had happened, and that feeling of being out of his body, watching what was going on and deciding he had to live. But the progressive removal of the drugs had changed his personality. Where before he had been kind and easygoing, now he would get angry with her over nothing. She was terrified the change would be permanent.

Dave Owen was a regular visitor. He had been back at the hospital the night of the rescue with another accident case, and been told that Mark was in the operating theatre with the odds stacked against him. Every time Dave went to the hospital he asked after Mark, until the day came when the ward sister said he was awake and talking and, 'Why don't you go and see him?'

Mark remembers not knowing what to say; 'thank you' did not seem to be enough. He gave him a hug and thanked him anyway. He wanted to know exactly what had happened and, as their friendship developed over the months, Dave had to describe what went on that night a hundred times.

Mark was finally allowed to leave hospital in late August, more than three months after the accident. Even then he faced more operations. He was to have fifteen over the next year and a half.

At first Sue thought it was like looking after two babies. She had to do the same things for Mark as she did for Ashley – help him wash, help him eat, support him as he tried to walk and listen to him as he learned to talk again.

Slowly he improved. He had to accept he would never play football again. He put all his cups and photos in a box and locked them away in the loft so as not to be reminded of how good he used to be.

It was more difficult to come to terms with never being a father again. The doctors had never been categorical about it, but they had thought the chances were very small.

So when Sue became pregnant it seemed a miracle all to itself. Michael was born two years after the accident, and they asked Dave Owen to be the godfather.

Life will never be the same for Mark. He still gets tired very easily; he has found it difficult to get a suitable job; just getting by is a struggle now. But, in other ways, the experience has made both him and Sue much stronger. They have been through so much; survived what most thought could not be survived. Mark can watch his children growing, thanks to the choice he still thinks he made that night watching the rescuers around his body in the wreckage.

Sue says the children make it all worth while, too. 'Two beautiful children who can see what a wonderful father they've got. Life's looking up.'

'Mark remembers not knowing what to say; "thank you" did not seem to be enough'

Dialling 999

Over 22 million emergency calls are made in Britain every year – many of them are dialled amid the panic and confusion of an accident. Although it's very upsetting to see people when they're injured and in distress (see page 19), it's important you remain calm, assess the situation and dial 999 knowing as much information as possible. Valuable time is wasted when callers cannot give accurate directions to the scene of an accident or when they are vague about exactly what has happened. By describing an incident clearly you can help ensure the emergency services arrive at the scene faster and better prepared.

The '999' call

'999' was first introduced in 1937 and is now probably the best-known telephone number in the country. You can dial 999 at any time of the day or night and from any telephone, including mobile phones. If there's an emergency and you're in a shop, supermarket, pub or restaurant don't be afraid to ask the manager to let you use the phone. Remember, all 999 calls are free. If you're in the street or in a park it may be quicker to ask to use the phone at the nearest cinema, garage or café rather than running to look for a call box. When you dial 999 your call is first answered at one of the thirty emergency operator centres in the country, before being connected to the appropriate emergency service as quickly as possible.

Calling for help

When your 999 call is answered, be ready to tell the operator which service you need. If you know someone has been injured always ask for the ambulance service even if you think you should call out the fire brigade and police too. You can also ask to be connected to the specialist rescue services – cave and mountain rescue, air–sea rescue, lifeboat and coastguard. The operator may ask you for the number of the phone you are calling from in case you are cut off. You will find this number either on the phone itself or, if you are in a call box, it's usually on a notice on the wall, together with the location of the call box. If the operator doesn't ask for your phone number, don't worry. New technology means that the numbers of nearly all 999 callers are displayed automatically and printed out so that the caller can be traced if they become unconscious or otherwise unable to talk. While the operator is ringing the emergency service you need, think of the clearest way to give the following information:

- WHAT HAS HAPPENED?

- WHERE HAS IT HAPPENED?

- WHO IS HURT OR ILL?

- HOW BADLY ARE THEY HURT?

- WHAT ABOUT OTHER DANGERS?

When you've given these brief details don't be tempted to hang up straight away – the emergency operator may need some more

WHY 999?

999 was originally chosen as the emergency service telephone number because it was easy to remember and simple to dial in the dark or a smoke-filled room. Today, with the increasing popularity of push-button phones, it's important to practise dialling 999 blindfold or with your eyes shut, on your own (unplugged) home phone. Remember, many phones have different key pads. Your home phone may have extra function buttons as well as the numbers, which could be confusing when you try to dial 999 in an emergency.

YOU CAN MAKE A CALL FROM ANY PHONE:

- Your own home telephone

- A public telephone

- A telephone in a pub, café, cinema or supermarket

- A mobile telephone

Remember
ALL 999 CALLS ARE FREE

NEVER MAKE A FALSE CALL:
It is against the law and could risk the lives of others who really need help.

information from you. Put the phone down only when the operator has done so. Remember, you only have to make one 999 call to ensure all the help you need arrives as quickly as possible. If an incident requires more than one emergency service, the others will be called by the service you are talking to.

False calls

More than half of the 999 calls made every year are false calls. Some are malicious hoaxes, but most are dialled by children. Never make a false call: it is against the law, and could risk the lives of others who really need help. And never allow very young children to play with the phone. Instead, make sure you explain to them the importance of the 999 call; children as young as four years old have been known to ring 999 and save their parents' lives. If you ever accidentally dial 999, do not hang up, but be ready to admit your mistake. It's vital you confirm that you do not require an emergency service. If you put the phone down without speaking, valuable time is then wasted tracing your call, in case it was a genuine cry for help. All 999 calls are now recorded to make sure vital details are not missed and to help sort out any problems that may occur later. The taping of calls also means they can be used as evidence in hoax call prosecutions.

HOW TO PHONE FOR HELP IN AN EMERGENCY

---

1 Lift the telephone handset and dial 999

---

2 Tell the operator the emergency service you need

Ambulance

Fire

Police

Mountain Rescue

Cave Rescue

Air–Sea Rescue

Lifeboat and Coastguard

---

3 Wait for the emergency service to answer

---

4 Give the following information

- WHAT HAS HAPPENED?

  road accident, bad fall, fire or drowning?

- WHERE HAS IT HAPPENED?

  number of building, name of street, nearby landmarks and useful directions

- WHO IS HURT OR ILL?

  how many people, their age and sex?

- HOW BADLY ARE THEY HURT?

  severe bleeding, head or spinal injuries, not breathing?

- WHAT ABOUT OTHER DANGERS?

  risk of fire or toxic fumes?

---

5 Don't hang up until the emergency service asks you to do so

CHAPTER 4
Killer in the House

Fire is the great domestic killer. There are so many things in every home that can start it, so many things to burn. Once it has taken hold it can leap and crackle through whole rooms in seconds.
By then it often doesn't matter; the killing has already been done by stealth.

It is the smoke that kills. We furnish our homes with materials that give off poison when they burn; the rooms fill with black smoke and lethal gases and we choke to death long before the flames reach us.

There are simple things we could do, but few of us bother. A little thought, a few simple precautions, could ensure our survival. But the figures go on rising: 65,000 house fires a year now, 600 dead, 10,000 injured. And there is nothing in the figures to describe the trauma people go through when their home and their security, everything they value, and often everybody they love, is being destroyed around them.

The fire that broke out in Sycamore Road, in the Handsworth district of Birmingham, one Saturday evening in January had all the ingredients of tragedy. The house was full of children. It might almost have been designed to trap them inside once the fire had taken hold. And the instinctive reactions of children and adults alike were to do the wrong thing, and put their lives even more at risk.

The speed and bravery of the firemen wouldn't have been enough to save them, without a broad slice of luck. In the end, the difference between life and death was about thirty seconds.

It was half-past six, and the large, extended family that lived there were scattered about the house. Kelon Khnam, who was twenty-one, and her younger sister Nahar, aged sixteen, were downstairs watching television. They had got a comedy programme on that the younger children either could not follow or did not like, so they had gone upstairs and found other things to do. The two girls' sister-in-law, Shamim Ara, was in the back bedroom on the first floor. She had said her prayers earlier that afternoon, and still had her prayer clothes on as she worked her way through a pile of ironing. With her in the room were her two sons, Rojon, who was seven, and Romun, five, and her baby daughter Shuria, who was then just a year old.

In the front room on the first floor were three more children: Shamim's two nephews, Shajamal, seven, and Shaalom, five, and her niece, Rita, nine. There were potential victims everywhere.

Nobody is sure *how* the fire started. They know *where* it started: in the cupboard on a small landing halfway up the staircase between the ground and first floors, which was used to store clothes.

Kelon smelt it first. Not all at once, more a gradual awareness of something catching at the back of her throat. At first she barely noticed it, but over ten minutes or so it got stronger and stronger; something she couldn't place. A smell of burning chemicals. A smell of danger.

She stepped out into the hall and immediately saw the fire halfway up the stairs. There were flames flickering and jumping in the billowing black smoke. She ran back and yelled at her sister to switch the television off and help her try to put it out. They got bowls of water from the kitchen to throw up the stairs.

It was hopeless. The fire was already long past the stage when it could be put out with buckets of water. The sisters were in a panic. All they could think of were the six children upstairs, beyond the flames. They thought it might still just be possible for them to come down, past the fire. They shouted and shouted, but couldn't make them hear. Every second, the flames were getting higher and stronger.

> 'The sisters were in a panic. All they could think of were the six children upstairs, beyond the flames'

Rita was doing her homework in the upstairs front room. Her brothers were being noisy; nobody had heard any sounds from downstairs. She could smell something and it kept distracting her from her work. She could not place it. She thought it might be the heater in the room. Several times she got up to see if there was something wrong with it. She noticed that each time she stood up the smell was worse, almost as if something plastic had been thrown on a bonfire. But there didn't seem to be anything wrong with the heater itself.

Eventually, she looked out on to the landing and what she saw set her screaming.

What happened then was so driven by panic that none of those involved can recall the exact sequence of events. Rita can remember her aunt, Shamim, coming out of her door and shouting, 'Oh, my God!' at the top of her voice.

Shamim, herself, remembers a period of terrible confusion. She knew she would not make it down the stairs. When she thought of it she could see a mental image of the flames racing up her sari. She gathered up her baby and her two young sons and went into the front room with the other children. She hoped she could open the window there to climb out, or at least call for help.

But when she got to it she found the window had been insulated with fixed, double-glazing. There was a slit for ventilation, and that was all. It did not open, and whatever she did she could not break it.

She could hear the roaring from the stairs. She was trapped with six children, and didn't know what to do.

She tried to gather the children together and get them to her room at the back of the building. But Rita's two brothers, Shaalom and Shajamal, were terrified by their first sight of the fire and did what children often do in these situations. They got away in the confusion and went back into their room to hide under their duvets. It is an instinctive reaction – they think that if they can't see the fire it will go away. It kills dozens of children every year, and was to come within seconds of killing Shaalom and Shajamal.

By now the greasy black smoke was making it difficult to see more than a yard or two, and almost impossible to breathe. Shamim managed to feel her way to her bedroom window. It was one of the few windows in the house that was not double-glazed. She had complained about it in the past; now it saved her life.

She heaved it open and screamed for help.

Two people heard her screams. The woman next door called the fire brigade. And the man over the road stopped just as he was turning his key in his front door.

Garnett Campbell had never heard a scream like it, just as if somebody was being murdered. He crossed the street to see what was happening, as people started shouting that the house was on fire.

The front door was open and he ran inside.

The heat, as he started to climb the stairs, was like a wall of pain. The landing by the cupboard was ablaze. He was blinded by the glare of the flames. Beyond was total darkness. The smoke that swirled around him was unlike anything he had ever seen before. It seemed almost solid; thick, and totally black. When he was in it, he reached forward to feel where he was going and could not see his hand. It choked him every time he took a breath.

He stopped short of the thickest smoke and thought for the first time of his own safety. What lay on the other side of this barrier of flames? And even if he got through, how would he ever get back? He would almost certainly be trapped himself, and die with anybody who was up there. In that moment he learned what firemen know from experience. On a burning staircase there is not much difference between a rescuer and a casualty.

The faces of his own children flashed through his mind. He turned and went back down the stairs to look for help.

In the kitchen he found the two sisters, Nahar and Kelon, on the edge of hysteria. They were just about able to tell him there were several children up on the first floor. Garnett tried to work out another way of getting to them. He wondered if his ladder would reach the windows, and ran back into the street.

Shamim was still at her window, clutching her baby and yelling for help. She could not tell if anybody had even heard her. All she did know was that the smoke was getting thicker and she could now feel the heat from the landing. She was worried about all the children, but her instinct was to save the baby first.

Through the smoke, she could see her sister-in-law, Kelon, in the back yard and she called down to her to look for an old mattress that the children had been playing with. But in the darkness and the confusion she did not understand. Shamim pushed herself further out on to the window ledge and made her decision. It did not matter what happened to her, the baby must survive. She prayed for a few seconds, and jumped.

She hit a chair as she landed, breaking her ankle and throwing her into the wall, which smashed her nose. She had managed to hold on to the baby and she did not have a scratch.

Now all Shamim could think about was the other children she had left behind. She tried to get up to look for the mattress, but her leg collapsed beneath her. She called up to them, begging them to jump, telling them, again and again, they would be burnt if they stayed any longer.

The older boy, Rojon, jumped first and she managed to catch him as he fell. The other two children left in the room were no longer able to breathe and were fighting with each other as they tried to get their heads out of the window for air. Romun gave Rita a shove that would have thrown her over the window ledge there and then, if her foot had not somehow been caught. She pulled it free and jumped. She, too, was safe.

Romun could not summon up the courage. He went as near to the edge as he dared. He hung on to the curtain outside the window as his mother pleaded with him to let go. Eventually, a blast of heat and smoke made up his mind for him. He fell safely into the garden.

Of the nine people in the house, seven were now safe. But it was all total confusion. Shamim was dragging herself across the back yard, crying for help. The children were having hysterics because they were convinced nobody left in the house could have survived. Smoke was pouring out of the upstairs windows, the staircase was

(Left) The open window from which five members of the family escaped. (Above) The cupboard on the landing at Sycamore Road, the source of the fire

in flames, and, somewhere inside, two little boys were hiding, hoping the fire would go away. The smoke was getting to them. They were choking under their bedclothes. They probably had a minute to live, two at the most, when the fire brigade arrived.

The night shift had just started at the Handsworth station when the message came in, logged at 18:32. They were warned what to expect. Four words in the jargon of the fire service chattering over the printer from headquarters: 'House fire. Persons Reported'. It is service shorthand to warn them that people might be trapped. It means they get there even faster than they do normally, making a lot of noise and not taking too much notice of red lights. It means somebody, somewhere, hasn't long to live. And that night it was right.

Both fire engines were turned out, each with the full crew of five firefighters struggling to get into their kit. Station officer Brian Cook was in the front of one of the appliances, alongside the driver. Firefighter Dave Darlinson was one of the three in the back. Two of the three were detailed to wear the full breathing apparatus for dangerous work in smoke-filled buildings. Tonight it was his turn. He fastened the face mask, and strapped on the air cylinders.

They turned into Sycamore Road at 18:35, and could see a crowd gathering outside the burning house. There was some smoke coming out of the bedroom windows at the front of the house. This one was not a hoax. Dave Darlinson clicked the air cylinders to 'on', and followed Brian Cook as he jumped down from the vehicle.

Just as they had pulled up, Garnett Campbell had run back across the road carrying his ladder under his arm. In the event, it would prove too short to be of any use but he obviously knew the way and Brian Cook and his men raced after him down the alleyway at the side of the house, saving valuable seconds.

The people in the back garden had been through a terrifying few minutes and it showed. Brian Cook found the children in great distress and Shamim collapsed in a heap in a corner of the yard. He could see her face was badly injured; her nose looked as if it had been almost ripped off. She was covered in blood and hardly knew where she was.

His priority was to find out if there was anybody else left in the building. It was not easy. Shamim grabbed hold of him and would not let him go. She was hysterical, and it was difficult to make out what she was saying. It took him a few moments to establish that there were some children left inside; he couldn't quite make out how many.

As the man in charge of the operation, his options had just narrowed considerably. He ordered Dave Darlinson and his mate, with the two breathing sets from the first appliance, to go in through the back of the house, and the men from the other appliance to go in the front. The instructions were simple; get upstairs and get the children out.

It is one of the most dangerous jobs a firefighter is called upon to do. To go up a blazing staircase that can collapse at any time; to walk through the flames and into the pitch darkness of a strange building; to search for a casualty by feel, knowing the seconds are ticking away and the longer it goes on the more likely you both are to end up dead.

Dave and his mate went in through the back door and made their way to the foot of the stairs. When they got there, two more firefighters, also wearing breathing apparatus, came in through the front door carrying a hose reel. The normal procedure would be to wait until the high pressure of water from the hose had damped down the fire before trying to climb the stairs. But they didn't have the time. They had to take the risk.

The flames had spread across the landing, along the banisters and up the walls by now. They were licking across the ceiling, melting the polystyrene tiles; molten lumps were dropping off and starting a series of smaller fires on the stair carpet.

The two firemen went up the stairs towards the main body of the fire. The landing was bright orange and red with flame; beyond was totally blotted out by the acrid black smoke. Nothing could stay alive in that for long.

Burning tiles fell on them as they climbed, but they brushed them off with their gloves. The heat was intense. Their flameproof suits gave them some protection; with all their gear on, the only place that really felt it was their ears. It would be their ears that would tell them they were pushing their luck too far.

They stepped quickly through the mouth of the fire on the half-landing and pushed on into the pitch darkness of the first floor.

It all depended now on training, bravery and luck – but mostly luck. They were effectively blind. They had no idea of the layout

'The landing was bright orange and red with flame; beyond was totally blotted out by the acrid black smoke' of the house, and no indication where the children might be. They had their own safety to consider. If their colleagues could not get the fire under control, they were going to be trapped, too.

The two split up at the top of the stairs. Dave went left, into the front bedroom, and his mate tried to find his way into the bedroom at the back.

Dave couldn't see anything when he stepped into the front room. He started to search it by feel, the way he had been trained. The instructors had told him children will always try to hide. Check in the beds, under the beds, in the wardrobes and cupboards and closets, under the furniture. That's where you will find them, or what's left of them.

He fumbled his way to the foot of the bed and almost immediately found Shajamal, who reared up from under the duvet, coughing desperately. He couldn't see him properly even when he was next to him, just a jerking outline in the dense smoke.

At the very moment he picked him up, the bedroom window was smashed from the outside by firemen who had put a ladder up against the front of the house. The timing was perfect. Dave handed the boy out of the window and turned back to look for his brother.

The open window had cleared the smoke slightly and Dave could see the silhouette of Shaalom at the other end of the bed. He was not breathing, but he was still alive. Dave grabbed him and pushed him as far out of the window, into the fresh air, as he could. Shaalom was passed down a chain of firemen, in the same way as his brother a few seconds before, and given oxygen in the back yard.

For those involved it had seemed an age, but the records show that it was barely five minutes from the 999 call to the moment when the last child was brought to safety. Even then, it was very nearly too late. If the fire engines had been held up, if the firemen had hesitated, if they had not split up at the top of the stairs so they could search both rooms at once, the boys would probably have been dead.

All the children were checked over in hospital and found to have suffered no lasting ill-effects. Shamim was treated for her facial injuries and the broken ankle, and allowed home a day or so later.

She was very scared when she went back. For weeks she thought she could sense smoke and fire and felt she couldn't breathe. When she closed her eyes she could imagine the fire as if it was still happening. For a long time she was too frightened to light the stove, or any of the fires in the house.

It was only when she saw her children again that she realized how lucky they all had been. She could not bear to think of losing any of them, nor of what would happen to the children if she had died. She still thanks God in her prayers, and the firemen who put their own lives at risk to save them.

The night shift at Handsworth station who put their lives at risk to save Shamim and her family

Fire Safety

The Handsworth fire could so easily have killed everybody in the house, and yet a few simple precautions would have ensured everybody's safety.

Night-time fires

The longer a fire goes undiscovered, the more dangerous it becomes. A fire at night, when people are sleeping, is three times more likely to kill than one during the day. Don't think the smoke will wake you or your pets up. The poisonous fumes given off by some modern furniture when it burns will kill you in your sleep.

Smoke detectors

Smoke detectors save lives. They cost only a few pounds. Just one will give you some warning, but it is much better to fit one in the hall, one on each landing, and one in any room where there's a chance fire might break out.

Buy smoke detectors that meet British Standard BS 5446. If they are mains-operated make sure they are fitted by a competent electrician. If battery-operated, replace the batteries every year (some models have a low battery warning bleep but many don't). Test your alarm about once a month to ensure it is in good working order.

Double glazing

The Handsworth house had double-glazing which didn't open wide enough for anybody to jump out. It can turn into a death trap. Don't fit double-glazing like this; if you have already got it, make sure there is a sharp, heavy implement nearby that you can use to break it if you need to escape. Hit the corner of the window – it will break more easily there than in the centre – and make safe any jagged edges by covering them with a towel or blanket.

How to Treat Burns

Remarkably, none of the inhabitants of the Handsworth house had to be treated for burns following the fire that so nearly ended their lives. But every year 600 people die and more than 10,000 patients suffering from burns are treated in our hospitals following house fires. The majority of victims are children and elderly people who are injured in preventable accidents within the home.

Most of us have a vague idea of what to do if someone burns or scalds themselves but there is so much folklore and so many half-truths about the right treatment to give, that many people actually do the wrong things and only make matters worse. There are a few simple rules for giving quick and correct first aid.

Minor burns and scalds

Small children are fascinated by steaming kettles or boiling pans. Accidents with hot liquids cause most burns and scalds in youngsters.

If it happens:

1 Remove source of heat, including any hot wet clothing.

2 Flood the burn with cold water for about 10 minutes (see left).

3 Gently remove any jewellery, watches or restrictive clothing.

4 Cover the burn with clean non-fluffy material (see below). A pure cotton sheet or cling film are good temporary coverings.

5 If worried, phone your doctor or local burns unit for advice.

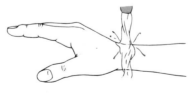
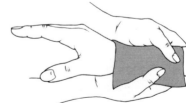

Getting out

Shamim Ara jumped from a first-floor window with her baby in her arms – miraculously the baby was completely unscathed although Shamim broke her ankle and smashed her nose. But remember, if you cannot get out on the ground floor don't jump from a first-floor window either. Lower yourself to arm's length and drop. Have children lowered down and never leave them until last.

Finally, a bit of forethought. Work out how you would get out of your home if there was a fire. And then work out an alternative route if, say, the staircase was ablaze. Make sure the whole family knows what to do, and practise it, preferably in the dark. Fire quickly disorientates you, even in your own home. You will not have a lot of time to get to safety.

Three simple things to remember if there's a fire in your home:

● Keep your head as close to the ground as possible to avoid the worst of the smoke.

● If a door feels warm to the touch, or if there is smoke coming underneath it, don't open it.

● And never, never, go back into the house once you have got out, even to collect valuables.

Three simple things to do to prevent a fire in your home:

● FIT A SMOKE ALARM AND TEST IT REGULARLY

● WORK OUT A FIRE ESCAPE PLAN AND PRACTISE IT REGULARLY

● CLOSE INTERIOR DOORS AT NIGHT

Get out

Stay out

Call the Fire Service out

You don't have to die

Clothing on fire

If you find someone whose clothes are on fire lay them down quickly. Put out the flames by starving them of oxygen. Either pour water over them or wrap the casualty tightly in a coat, blanket or rug to smother the flames. Don't use any man-made material, like nylon, which may melt and stick to the skin making the burn more serious. Only try to put out the flames by rolling the casualty on the floor if you've no alternative because there's a danger it will actually spread the flames and burns further.

But if you're alone and your clothes are on fire, don't panic and run about as this will fan the flames and make things worse. The advice is to stop, drop to the floor and keep rolling over until the flames are out – stop, drop and roll.

Smoke inhalation

People who have escaped from a house fire may have inhaled fumes. Breathing in smoke, gases or toxic vapours from burning plastics, foam in furniture, and synthetic wall coverings can be fatal. Smoke or fumes that accumulate in a confined space can quickly overcome anyone, including a would-be rescuer who is not wearing protective equipment. *Do not* go into a smoke-filled room without proper safety apparatus. Anyone who has inhaled smoke needs urgent medical attention. First of all call 999, asking for both the ambulance and fire services. If the casualty is unconscious check for breathing and pulse and be prepared to resuscitate if necessary. If they are breathing and there is a pulse, place in the recovery position. When the ambulance arrives the casualty will usually be given oxygen. People who have been trapped in a smoke-filled room may also have burns to the mouth or throat. Usually there are certain tell-tale signs: swelling of the lips, soot around the nose, coughing and spluttering as well as breathing difficulties. These burns are dangerous as they cause rapid swelling of the airways leading to a serious risk of suffocation, so always seek medical help in these cases. You can try to cool down these internal burns by getting the casualty to sip cold water or suck an ice cube, but watch very closely to ensure they do not choke if swallowing becomes difficult.

CHAPTER 5

Whirlpool

Hayley Rogers is proud of her hair, even though it looks a bit odd now. Even though it so nearly killed her.

Hayley was twelve when she was involved in a freak accident nobody dreamt could happen. Even now, it is difficult to imagine how a strong swimmer like her nearly died in a children's pool, surrounded by lifeguards, on a crowded bank holiday weekend.

Hundreds of people could reach her; but it took two flashes of inspiration and a lot of skill to save Hayley's life.

The Rogers family had been undecided about the Easter holiday. They had been keen on the idea back at the beginning of March when the summer, as it often does, seemed to have arrived early. But in the week leading up to Easter winter was back and the weather was spiteful. The children wanted to go, particularly as the plan was to meet up at a caravan park in Hampshire with another family they had met on holiday the year before. It was the leisure centre down the road from the caravans that proved to be the deciding factor. It would be a shame if the weather was bad. But at least there would be something for the kids to do.

Good Friday morning started with a disappointment for the children. The holiday tradition, especially when they were camping or in a caravan, was the big fry-up breakfast. But Margaret Rogers was a Catholic; she felt it was wrong to eat meat on Good Friday. Despite their protests, she gave them boiled eggs and toast.

It was one of the crazy things that were to pass through her mind later that day – a feeling of relief that she hadn't given in that morning. As if God would not have let Hayley live if she had eaten a sausage on Good Friday.

It was not actually raining, but it was miserable enough for the parents to realize their plan of going to the beach would have to be postponed until the afternoon. The children preferred the idea of the leisure centre, anyway.

They were impressed when they got there. Swimming pools, sauna, arcades, restaurant. Between the two families there were seven children, aged two to fifteen. It was never easy to keep them all amused, but it didn't seem to be any problem that morning. The kids and their dads were in the water for hours. It was warm in the main pool, perhaps because it was getting rather crowded. And they all liked the children's whirlpool. It was shallow, barely four feet deep. But a pump sucked the water in a circle, so it felt like a real whirlpool. And it was safe. Even the two-year-old went in.

While they were having lunch at the leisure centre it started pouring with rain: a typical English bank holiday day. The parents still wanted to go to the seaside, but there was no point in going until it stopped. The children drifted off to the amusement arcades and came back. It was still raining. They started to get bored and eventually, inevitably, began to be a bit of a nuisance. They wanted to go back in the water. The weather was looking worse and worse.

There didn't seem to be any point in saying no. The parents gave up the idea of the beach and fresh air. It was the sort of day leisure centres are built for.

Hayley didn't mind the weather at all. As far as she and her friend, Pippa Bonnefoy, were concerned, the swimming pool was great fun. They didn't mind if they never went to the beach.

It was late afternoon when they decided to take a break from the main pool. It was crowded, and it was hot. The children's whirlpool was different. They had discovered already it was a good place to cool down.

The girls normally tied their hair up when they were swimming, but neither had bothered that day. Besides, it was fascinating watching it spread out in the whirlpool when they ducked their heads under to cool off.

This time when they knelt down in the pool and leant back to put their heads in the water, Hayley felt a sharp tug on her hair. She thought somebody else had got into the pool and stepped on it. She tried to pull away, tried to break free, all the while thinking that whoever it was would realize they were treading on her hair and get off, and let her raise her head out of the water. She turned to see what was happening and saw the tangle of her hair disappearing into a round, plastic grid. She grabbed her hair and started pulling. She kicked against the walls with her feet, and waved desperately with her arms. Why hadn't anybody noticed her?

Pippa was still lying back in the water when Hayley suddenly kicked her in the head. She reared up out of the water and was going to have a go at her. But she wasn't playing. She was struggling in the water, thrashing wildly about.

Pippa could not work out what was happening at first. Hayley was face down in the water, tugging at her head. She seemed to be stuck, but Pippa could not see how. She pulled on her legs, and when that did not work she grabbed her by the hips and heaved at them. But nothing she did had any effect. She stepped back and started to scream.

One breath, that's all she wanted. If she could only get one breath, Hayley thought, she could stay alive. And it was so close. The surface was only inches away. She could see it, even though the chlorine was stinging her eyes. If only she had Pippa's hair, she thought. It's longer, long enough to just get her face clear of the water; long enough to get that one breath; long enough to let her live.

Whenever she stopped struggling the grille seemed to pull her down, closer to the bottom and further from the surface where she yearned to be.

There was such a crowd around the pool, and they were all making so much noise, that for a few, terrible moments nobody took any notice of Pippa. Suddenly everybody started yelling at once, and the lifeguards arrived.

John Gething was proud of his job. He was seventeen, and had been doing it for only five days. He was lucky to have that kind of job at his age. When he had finished his bronze lifesaving course a couple of months before he had thought he would have to wait a lot longer before he got a chance to put it into practice. He could not have been more wrong.

It had been a tiring day. There were probably more than a hundred people in the main pool. It was warm and humid and some of the kids were being a pain. He had been down to the spa bath telling Nathan Dowse, the other lifeguard, that it was getting crowded at his end. They had split up because he had had to go and tell a group of young children, for what must have been the twentieth time that day, to stop breaking the rules when he heard the shouting over at the whirlpool.

His boss, Craig Alston, was in the reception area, catching up with his paperwork. There had been a lot of shouting that day, but this time it was something different, something that made him look up from his work, something that made him run for the door. There's a difference between excitement and panic. An edge to the raised voices; an urgency in the screams.

He ran out to the poolside and saw John and Nathan jumping into the whirlpool. He was only a couple of yards behind them.

John did not realize Hayley was stuck. He thought she had banged her head, and was lying there unconscious. He tried to lift her out of the water, but she just felt like a log.

The three of them took hold of her. Three strong men, and still she did not move. It was like trying to pull a brick out of a wall with your bare hands, he thought. Worse, it was as if she was stuck to the bottom with superglue.

In the confusion he heard Craig shouting she was trapped. He

> 'There's a difference between excitement and panic. An edge to the raised voices, and urgency in the screams'

999 John, Nathan and Craig tried to wrench Hayley free, but she was stuck fast

had ducked his head under the water and seen her hair caught up in one of the intake valves. The swirling water had plaited her hair into what was effectively a thick strand of rope that now tied her by the head to the bottom of the whirlpool. He yelled at the other two to pull harder, hoping it would tear loose. But they couldn't move her at all.

There had to be another way. She couldn't just die like this, with all of them standing around. Craig jumped out of the pool to go and switch off the pumps, leaving John and Nathan still trying to wrench Hayley free.

When everybody started jumping in the pool Hayley calmed down for a moment. They're going to get on with it, she thought. Everything seemed to go into fast-forward. 'It's going to be over quickly. They're going to rip my hair out by the roots and I won't care – just so long as they get me out.' She saw a man's leg and she grabbed hold of it, trying to pull herself up to the surface. She felt hands taking hold of her arms, her legs, her waist, even round her neck. She thought: 'They're going to break every bone in my body, but I don't care, if they can just get me out of this.'

She tried to hold her breath. Her body felt as if it were swelling up to an enormous size, making itself bigger and bigger to get more oxygen in. She tried to let out only a little bit of air at a time. It felt like her ears were going to burst and her stomach was going to explode. Her underwater world started to go blurred.

John Gething could not believe what was happening. There was never any problem in the children's whirlpool. Once or twice you would have to tell kids off for jumping in, but it was the safest place in the centre. Now it was full of people screaming their heads off.

He wondered what else was caught, as well as her hair. She was so rooted into the bottom of the pool he had visions of her hands trapped in the intake, her arms maybe.

He ducked his head under for another look, and when he came back up again his eye was caught by a woman in the crowd by the edge of the pool. A middle-aged woman with blonde hair, shouting at the top of her voice. She was in a panic, yelling at him, 'She can't breathe. She can't breathe. She can't *breathe!*'

That's when it hit him. He stood motionless for a moment. For the first time he realized the girl was going to die there and then if she couldn't get some air, somehow. He also realized that it was all down to him.

All the training came back to him then, the way they said it would. It seemed natural. He pushed his head into the water and pulled her head round. He put his mouth over hers and tried to do mouth-to-mouth resuscitation.

But however hard hard he tried he didn't seem to be able to get any air into her. He had only ever practised the technique on dry land. When he tried it under water he could not get a seal around her mouth. The bubbles, the air on which her life depended, just escaped past his cheeks, back up to the surface. She had started thrashing around again and her eyes stared at him each time he went back down to her. And each time he went back to the surface he saw the same woman's face, frozen in panic.

It wasn't working.

It was no longer going fast-forward. To Hayley it seemed now as if the tape had been rewound and was now being played in slow motion. Everything seemed to be coloured in misty browns and blacks. It was getting dark. She was hallucinating. In the darkness she could see a grave, and she could even read her name on it. She could see her mother and father, her brother and her sister kneeling round the grave and crying. She thought: 'I've got to get out or they'll shout at me.'

It had been a shock when somebody had grabbed her by the jaw. It had been such a sharp tug and she had not expected it. Whoever it was pulled her face round and pinched her nose. For a moment she relaxed. He's going to get me out now because he knows what to do. He's going to get me free, or at least he's going to keep me alive until someone else gets me out. She was relieved to know she did not have to hold on any more. That he could breathe for her – live for her – and she would be able to carry on and live her life.

Such a relief that her mother would not be standing by her grave, or shouting at her.

The noise was going now. All the shouting and screaming was going away. The people were disappearing. Everything was blurring into nothingness. The colours were melting into each other. It was getting darker and darker, until it was black and she was gone.

John Rogers was waiting in the reception area for his wife to come back from the car. He had not seen Hayley for quite a while, but she was big enough to look after herself. The two little ones wanted to go in again, and he'd decided to go in with them as soon as his wife came back with the costumes.

As he glanced through the glass window at the pool his eyes were caught by the crowd. There was something, he did not know what, that made him turn to a man near him and say, 'What's going on?'

He was a shy man. It wasn't what he would do normally. The man said he thought there was somebody in trouble. Something was nagging away in John Rogers's mind. Something that made him push his way through the crowd to the whirlpool.

He saw Pippa. She was crying and was being held by a woman he did not recognize. He searched hard for Hayley but could not see her anywhere, until he had got to the edge of the whirlpool.

It was the hair that he saw first. It seemed to him then that the pool was full of it. Fine hair, like when you bath a baby and its wispy hair spreads across the surface of the water.

He doesn't know whether he shouted. He froze by the side of the pool. One of the crowd. But the victim was his daughter.

Craig Alston ran back to the pool thinking he had solved the problem. He had switched the pumps off that drew the water down through the intake valves. There was no more suction, so when he jumped back into the whirlpool he expected her to come up straight away.

But she didn't.

He pulled her. They all pulled her. They had been very aware of hurting her at first. They hadn't wanted to pull her hair out. But now she must have been under two minutes or more and their efforts to tear her free became fierce. It did not matter if they scalped her if they could only save her life. When they got to the point where they risked breaking her bones because of the force they were using, Craig called a halt. The only way was to cut her out.

His mind raced round trying to think of what he could use. There were no diving knives, or anything like that in the centre. All he could think of was the tiny scissors in the first-aid box in reception. Nathan brought them and he started cutting. But by this time her hair had twirled round and formed a rope maybe two inches thick. The scissors made little impression on it. He knew she would be long dead by the time he cut her free; but he had no choice.

John Gething looked down at her and thought she looked like a ghost on a dark night. She was so white under the sheen of water she looked like a spirit in the moonlight.

He knew he was her lifeline. But he knew, too, that the mouth-to-mouth resuscitation was not working. He doesn't know how it came into his mind. He suddenly remembered from his course how they gave artificial respiration to babies. You had to get their nose in somehow. It would be different with an older child, but if he tried to get the air into her nose, rather than her mouth . . .

999 John Gething '. . . tried to get the air into her nose rather than her mouth . . .'

He tried it. Then he tried it again. It seemed to be working because this time the bubbles didn't rush past his face the way they had when he had tried to blow air into her mouth. Now he could get a decent seal around her nose, force the air into her, keep her nose pinched tightly shut when he went up for another breath, and so on.

Each time he came up for air — one gulp for him and one for the girl — he could see Craig at work with a pair of scissors. It seemed very slow. He thought to himself: If I give up, she'll die. He did not know if it was the right thing to do. He did not know how long he could keep going, But he, too, had no choice.

It was Paul Noble's inspiration that saved her life. He was a member at the leisure centre, and had done training as a diver medic. When the panic started he had helped hold the crowd back, to give the lifeguards room to work. Now he could see Craig trying to cut through the girl's hair with the scissors from the first-aid box. That's not going to work, he thought. Those scissors are nearly always blunt and rounded at the edges.

Like everybody else there, he heard Craig shouting for a knife. The difference was, he thought he knew where to find one.

His training told him every second was vital. He covered the forty yards or so at a run, hurling people out of his way. He was heading for the club, the restaurant and bar area. He had been in the bar a couple of nights before and, in his mind's eye he could see the big serrated knife they used to cut lemons for the drinks.

The place was packed. People were three deep at the bar. Paul ran in, yelling at them to get out of the way. Someone shouted, 'It's a raid!' The bar staff were screaming. Tables and chairs went over. The crowd opened up and Paul vaulted the bar. He snatched the knife, rolled over the bar, and was on his way back to the pool, leaving chaos behind him. It had taken no more than a few seconds. If it had taken any more, things might well have been different.

On his way back he barged into Margaret Rogers. She still had no idea what was happening. She had come back from the car with the swimming things and heard people saying that somebody had their head stuck in the swimming pool. She was walking down the corridor to the pool when she was almost knocked over by a man carrying what she thought was a carving knife. Goodness, she thought, they're surely not going to cut his head off? and told herself off for being ridiculous.

Back at the pool Paul saw Craig still cutting away with his scissors, getting nowhere. He screamed at him to take the knife. Craig threw away the scissors and dived back under the water. With the knife it took only a few seconds to slice through all her hair and cut her free. They pulled her up, but could not tell whether all they had freed was a dead body. She had been under water well over four minutes. She had stopped struggling long ago and was obviously not breathing.

John Gething had never seen somebody look like that. She had bright purple lips. She was bloated and her skin had the grey tinge of cyanosis, oxygen starvation. She looked and felt like a corpse.

'They couldn't believe it. It seemed to them like a miracle. One minute she was dead; the next she was lying there crying from the shock of what had happened to her'

Craig knew they had to be very quick. He went straight for her mouth, while John checked her heart. He gave her two breaths of mouth-to-mouth resuscitation and she started to cough. They couldn't believe it. It seemed to them like a miracle. One minute she was dead; the next she was lying there crying from the shock of what had happened to her.

Panic hit Margaret Rogers like a brick wall. Where was Hayley? Somebody's head is stuck in the swimming pool and there's a man with a carving knife, and why isn't Hayley there? Her husband seemed to fly through the door and everything went into slow motion for her.

'It's Hayley, Marg,' he said, 'but they're saying she's all right.' Everything went blank for her then, until she was looking down at her daughter, thinking she was dead. They had put her in the recovery position, but all Margaret could see was the unnatural white of her body, her purple face, and the staring eyes, protruding out of her head.

She threw herself on to the floor beside her and, as she did so, could feel her breathing. But she was still absolutely motionless; she did not say anything and the eyes did not blink.

Everybody around her was saying she was going to be all right, but she didn't believe them. Even if she lives, she thought, her brain will be damaged.

Over and over she said, 'Hayley, it's Mummy, Hayley, it's Mummy, talk to me,' but she did not reply.

Then she blinked, and spoke. 'I'm sorry, Mum, I'm sorry.' Her mother cried and held her, and felt it was just like the minute she had been born – all over again.

She stroked her hair, and it came away in handfuls. She can remember looking up at the lifeguards, who were totally exhausted – John in particular, the one they said had saved her life by giving her resuscitation under water. He didn't look any bigger than Hayley. He looked, she thought, as if he needed a mum himself. She asked him how he was, and he burst into tears.

Even so, John felt he had somehow grown up. That he had found within himself a skill and maturity he did not know he had. When the crunch came he had not panicked. Something inside him had taken over, some inner remote control had switched on, and he did what had to be done.

Anyway, everybody else was crying, the tension had been so great and the relief so overwhelming.

Hayley can remember the first thing she knew was her body was itching all over. Then she began to see again. The process was the exact reverse of drowning. Everything started to get lighter and, gradually, more and more in focus. She could not stop apologizing for causing everybody trouble.

For Craig, the best thing was not having to tell a mother: 'Sorry, your daughter's dead.' Instead, they were talking about how she could have her hair permed, how they both hoped it would not put her off swimming.

It could so easily have been different.

Hayley was checked over in hospital, but the experience had done no lasting damage. She was bruised all over, but the bruises soon went. The hair is taking longer to grow back, and gets on her nerves until she thinks what would have happened to her if it had not been cut off. She still goes swimming, but will never forget to tie her hair back again.

They have changed the system in the whirlpool. Water is now pumped into the pool, not out of it and is removed by a simple overflow.

It was a freak accident, but they don't want any chance of it happening again.

John (left) and Craig with Hayley whom they hoped had not been put off swimming by her accident

ABC of Resuscitation

If someone stops breathing it is vital to get air into the lungs as soon as possible – a delay in breathing of just a few minutes will result in severe brain damage. A delay of more than six minutes can cause death. First-aid experts say it's always better to have a little knowledge and do something

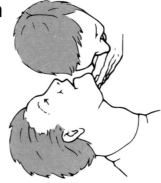

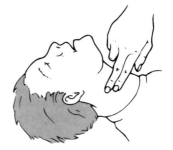

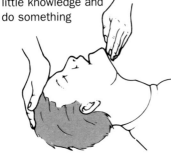

in an emergency rather than do nothing and wait for help to arrive. You can help save the life of a casualty who appears unconscious by knowing the ABC of resuscitation.

AIRWAY – Open the airway by tilting the head and lifting the chin (see left) and carefully removing any obstructions from the mouth to allow air, containing oxygen, to flow into the lungs.

BREATHING – Check for breathing by looking to see if the chest is rising and falling, as well as listening and feeling for breath on your cheek (see above). Someone who is not breathing may have a bluish tinge to the lips and face and will need immediate artificial ventilation.

CIRCULATION – Check for a pulse in their neck or wrist.

If there is a pulse and they are breathing put them in the recovery position (see below).

If there is a pulse and no breathing commence mouth-to-mouth resuscitation (see below).

If there is no pulse and no breathing someone must phone for an ambulance immediately, and then carry out a combination of chest compressions (see overleaf) and mouth-to-mouth.

Recovery position (see left) Turn the casualty on to their side. Keep their head tilted with their chin forward to keep the airway open. Check that they cannot roll over. Check their breathing and pulse frequently. If either stops follow the ABC of resuscitation.

Mouth-to-mouth resuscitation is the simplest and most effective method of introducing air into the lungs. Kneel by the casualty. Keep the head tilted fully back and pinch the nose closed. Take a deep breath and seal your mouth completely over the casualty's mouth. Breathe slowly into their mouth, watching their chest rise. Let the chest fall completely before giving a second breath. Continue blowing into the lungs at the rate of ten breaths per minute until you see the victim beginning to breathe alone.

Mouth-to-nose resuscitation may be used when the casualty is being supported in water or when the mouth is injured so that you can't get a firm seal. As with mouth-to-mouth ventilation, open the airway by tilting the head back and lifting the chin. Take a deep breath and seal your mouth around the victim's nose. Blow strongly into the nose. Remove your mouth and hold the victim's mouth open with your hand, so that air can escape. Repeat as for mouth-to-mouth resuscitation every six seconds.

Chest compressions

It is important to make sure the casualty is on a firm surface and to give two breaths of artificial respiration before beginning chest compressions. Press with the heel of one hand placed on top of the other. It is vital to apply pressure at the correct point – the lower part of the breastbone. Do not press down any more than one and a half to two inches and keep the pressure well clear of the casualty's ribs. If you are on your own, do this at a rate of eighty per minute, stopping to give two breaths after every fifteen compressions. If there are two rescuers, one should carry out the chest compressions at the same rate as before, and the other mouth-to-mouth at the rate of one breath to every five compressions. When the pulse returns,

immediately stop the compression. Once breathing starts, put the casualty in the recovery position. NEVER attempt compressions if the heart is beating.

Although it is possible to get someone breathing again in an emergency by following the above

instructions, to restore the circulation if the heart has stopped beating (chest compressions) cannot be learned effectively from a book during an emergency. Ideally you should learn how to do this on a first-aid course and then practise the technique regularly. You are also recommended to regularly refresh your skills so that you will always be prepared in the event of an emergency. Remember, most accidents happen in the home or on journeys, so it's very likely that the person you may have to help will be someone in your family or someone you know.

FIRST-AID TRAINING AGENCIES

British Heart Foundation
14 Fitzhardinge Street
London W1H 4DH
tel. 071-935 0185

British Red Cross
9 Grosvenor Crescent
London SW1X 7EJ
tel. 071-235 5454

Order of Malta Ambulance Corps
83 University Street
Belfast BT7 1HP
tel. 0232-245373

Resuscitation Council (UK)
9 Fitzroy Square
London W1P 5AH
tel. 071-388 4678

Royal Life Saving Society UK
Mountbatten House
Studley
Warwickshire B80 7NN
tel. 0527-853943

St Andrew's Ambulance
Association
St Andrew's House
48 Milton Street
Glasgow G4 0HR
tel. 041-332 4031

St John Ambulance
1 Grosvenor Crescent
London SW1X 7EF
tel. 071-235 5231

The NHS Ambulance Service also offer courses: please look in the telephone directory and contact the headquarters of your local NHS Ambulance Service.

Also the Health and Safety Executive have registered trainers for training employees in first aid for the legal health and safety at work requirements. Contact their information centre at
Broad Lane,
Sheffield S3 7HQ
tel. 0742 892345

CHAPTER 6

Fighting with Fear

Johnny O'Keefe was not feeling at all well that morning. It was a tough life on the building site, out in all weathers, and he was not as young as he was. But that morning, cold and blustery even though it was July and meant to be summer, was different somehow. He couldn't put his finger on it. He just did not feel right.

Steve Puhlhofer (left) and Nigel Firkins face up to the task ahead

He found a parking space near the site. Always the most difficult job of the day, he thought to himself. It was still only seven in the morning, but a place to park in that busy part of Uxbridge was as rare as a foreman with married parents. Twenty-seven years he had worked on the cranes. You would think you would be used to the early starts by now, he told himself. Come on, get going.

He looked around the site for his mate and was relieved to see big Patsy Mitchell was already there. It was hell when you had to work on your own. He and Patsy took it in turns to drive the big crane that soared 180 feet over the building site and dominated the skyline of west London. One would work the cab, right at the top of the crane; the other would be on the ground as banksman, sorting out the jobs and keeping in touch by two-way radio.

They decided Johnny would go up for the first shift. His chest was hurting a bit, but it was probably only a cold. You got lots of them on a building site and if you were to stop work every time you had a sniffle you would never work again. He headed off to start the long, lonely climb to the top of the crane. It took so long to get all the way up there your mate had time to go for breakfast before the work started.

Patsy wondered for a moment about him as he watched him walk away. Johnny was normally such a chirpy, pleasant sort of man; the sort of good humour that could really shorten the day. Early morning blues, probably, something on his mind. He would cheer up soon. He always did.

The base of the crane was twenty-five feet below ground, so Johnny had to climb down a ladder and cross what would become the basement car park of the new building before he could reach the bottom of the tower and start climbing. He was getting too old for this, he thought. When he was young he could have climbed to the top without a break. But these days he was grateful for the little platforms, every fifty feet or so, where he could have a few minutes' rest. The way he felt that morning, even getting to the first one would be a struggle.

By the time he reached it he was feeling really bad. He was tired all over, and there was a peculiar tightness in his chest. London looked quiet and peaceful, the way it always did from up there at half-past seven in the morning. But it was starting to move, in and out like somebody playing a trombone. The tower was getting narrower and narrower. He said to himself, out loud, 'What's wrong with me?'

The whole of London seemed to be shrinking, disappearing into a tiny dot, as if the real world was a television set and someone had switched it off. This is what it is like to die, he thought. He did not think of his family or his home or his friends. It was happening so fast he just thought: That's it, it's over. He can remember saying, 'What a bloody awful place to die.' There, on a narrow ledge not much bigger than the soles of his feet, fifty feet over a building site.

He blacked out.

When he came to, he was a hundred feet further up, on the bell platform just under the cab, breathtakingly high above London. He has never been able to explain how he got there, how he climbed all that way up a dangerous ladder, after he had apparently lost consciousness.

He knew straightaway something was seriously wrong. 'How the hell did I get here?' he thought and, almost at once, the pains began. They were all over his chest and his neck, and down both arms. It was a narrow platform, not a great deal bigger than the ledge where he had passed out, far below. His immediate fear was that he would lose consciousness again and fall down the ladder, all the way down the long, straight, row of metal bars, that stretched unbroken all the way to the ground.

He was left-handed, so he tried to move that arm first, but it was paralysed. He could move the right arm, though, and grabbed the first thing he could find, which turned out to be a bunch of live cables. He wrapped them, tight, round his right wrist. He didn't mind the risk of electrocuting himself. All he cared about was, if he passed out again, he would hang there by his wrist and not fall to his death.

Down below Patsy Mitchell was getting impatient. It was always the same, first thing. Everybody wanted the crane for some vital lift or other that had to be done right away or the whole site would be held up for hours. How much longer was it going to take for Johnny to drop the chains and get going? He must have been gone twenty minutes or more.

Patsy had been around a long time. You didn't rush a man at the

'When he came to, he was a hundred feet further up, on the bell platform just under the cab, breathtakingly high above London. He has never been able to explain how he got there'

start of the day. Particularly a crane driver who could wipe out dozens of people with one mistake. And especially not a man like Johnny. You eased a man into his day's work, if he was not feeling on top form. If he wanted to study form for a minute or two, have a cigarette, while his heart stopped thumping from the long climb, that was fine. The last thing you wanted to do was upset him. Still, this was getting ridiculous. He picked up the two-way radio.

Johnny could not tell how long he had been there, half lying, half hanging from the cables, when the radio started crackling somewhere above his head. They left it permanently switched on in the cab, and through it he could hear Patsy shouting to him, 'Johnny, what's the matter? Can't you start? Have you got power? What the hell's wrong?'

Typical, Johnny thought. All hell let loose down there. Everybody wants the crane and look at me, lying here. He tried to move but he couldn't. His limbs were rigid, and all down his left side felt numb. It was only four steps up the trapdoor into the cab, but it might just as well have been on the moon. There was no way he could get there, no way he could get to the radio.

The only thing he could do to signal them down below was to edge himself slightly sideways and push his right hand out through the framework of the crane and waggle it about. If they were looking hard they might just see it.

It needed keen eyes to spot a man's hand, nearly two hundred feet up in the sky, but Patsy spotted it. Johnny could hear him over the radio: 'There's something wrong – look, can you see him, thrown down on the floor under the cab. Look, you can see his hand.'

Someone was saying he couldn't see anything, and they started arguing about it. Johnny could hear every word, but he couldn't move any more. He had never felt so bad, so helpless.

He heard Patsy say he was going up to see what was going on, but he must have blacked out again, because the next thing he knew was Patsy's face poking up through the ladder, looking worried.

'I'm conked out, Patsy,' he said. 'Something terrible's wrong with me. I can't move a limb, I've had it.'

Patsy got on the radio to call for help, and settled down with him to wait. He looked at Johnny and wondered how they would ever get him down.

Rhythm, that was how to do it. Rhythm and always looking out, not down.

Heights had never really bothered Nigel Firkins before. You couldn't be a firefighter if you were scared of going up a ladder. In the training they had made him crawl off the end of a turntable ladder that had been extended pretty well to its full length. It had been scary, but he had handled it. The crane was worse, much worse, but he would handle this, too.

From the bottom, the crane had seemed to stretch to infinity. He couldn't really see the top. As he climbed, he kept telling himself it wasn't heights that were the problem, it was falling off that was the problem. Once you are over thirty feet or so, it did not really matter how high you went anyway; if you fell off you'd had it. Rhythm, concentration, training.

He would make it, but wondered about the young ambulanceman coming up behind him.

Steve Puhlhofer didn't like it at all. He had started the climb for the sake of the patient. It was what he was trained to do, what he had always done: put the patient first.

But he had only gone a few feet when the fear hit him like a punch in the stomach.

For the first time in his life, he didn't care about the patient, couldn't even think about him. All he cared about was his own, overwhelming terror. He felt hot and dizzy. His body seemed weak even though he could see how tightly he was hanging on to the ladder. His knuckles really were white. He could feel his pounding heartbeat radiating out into his hands.

It was the fear that, somehow, kept him going. He did not want to go up, but he did not want to go down either. Or stay where he was. All he wanted was somebody to take him off that ladder and lower him to the ground.

That was his frame of mind, before the incident that nearly killed him.

He had not been able to take much equipment with him, just the resuscitation pack on his back with oxygen, some airways, and an artificial respirator. The pack had two hooks on the top for attaching it to a stretcher. Halfway up the ladder, achingly high above London, the hooks caught on the safety rail.

Steve thought someone had grabbed him and was trying to pull

'He had only gone a few feet when the fear hit him like a punch in the stomach'

him off the ladder. He felt a hot surge through his shoulder and his feet skidded off the rungs. He had already been hanging on for dear life; now he felt himself go. He was falling, and there would be nothing to stop him until he hit the ground.

In fact he slipped no more than a couple of rungs before his grasping hands and his scrabbling feet managed to stop him. But he felt totally destroyed. He had been so scared anyway, and his confidence was never more than paper thin. The sudden jerk, the brief certainty that he was falling all the way, finished him off. He hugged the ladder and his mind went completely blank.

His senses came back slowly, and with them the realization that he was still caught by the hooks on his resuscitation pack. It seemed an age before he could bring himself to take one hand off the ladder to free himself. A quick, desperate, movement with a hand wet with sweat, and he was hanging on with both hands again, cuddling the ladder for all he was worth, knowing he must look utterly ridiculous from down there on the ground, but beyond caring.

After a while he tried to move, but it was as if he was glued there. He tried to talking to himself, working it out logically. He could not go down. He was too scared to and, in any case, he could not face the shame of it. He could not stay where he was, however much his body kept telling him that was all he could do. The only place to go was up.

He tried not to look down. He took a few deep breaths, and moved his hand up to the next rung.

The ground was disappearing beneath him. All he could see, across the city, seemed unreal and his mind kept confusing the movement down below with his own movements, making him dizzy. He felt hot, and there was a huge pressure inside him, as if he was going to burst. He tried to concentrate on looking at his hands, as he moved them slowly, rung after rung. But he could not conquer his fear. He felt alone up in the sky, vulnerable and absolutely petrified.

By this time the fireman, Nigel Firkins, had reached the bell platform. He found Johnny O'Keefe sprawled in the corner. Nigel did not need his first-aid training to know that he was in a bad way. His face had a ghostly pallor and, though he tried to speak, his words were slurred and did not make much sense. There was a look in his eyes, too. Nigel had seen it before, in the eyes of people who did not think they were going to live much longer.

He asked him his name, and made an effort to reassure him. He tried to think of a way to get him down to the ground. They may have been in the middle of London, but they were all on their own up there, on a cramped little platform, shaking and wobbling in a stiff westerly breeze. It wouldn't be easy.

Most of all he wondered where the ambulanceman had got to. The way the casualty was looking, there might not be much time.

Steve Puhlhofer was shaking uncontrollably as he pulled himself on to the platform. He dared not look around. He could not bring himself to look at the fireman, at Patsy Mitchell, or even the casualty. His training was all forgotten. He just dropped on to all fours, frozen with the relief of having a floor between him and the ground. He was convinced that if he tried to move he would be sucked off the side of the platform and that would be the end.

Semi-conscious though he was, Johnny O'Keefe knew what Steve was going through. He had seen brave men start gibbering at this height. Even crane drivers had to get acclimatized; it took him a week or so to get used to it again after his summer holidays. It needed a special kind of courage to carry on when you felt that way, he thought. He tried to focus on the lad, and for a moment their eyes met.

He really was very sick, Steve thought, and it somehow kicked him into gear. This man was going to die if he didn't do something. He crawled over to him on all fours for a closer look.

He was pale and clammy; his breathing was shallow, his eyes were barely open and he was mumbling incoherently – all the signs of a major heart attack. Funny, Steve thought, he himself seemed to have most of the same symptoms. He tried to calm down; he was shaking so much he thought he would shake himself right off the side of the crane. He felt for Johnny's heartbeat, but all he could feel was his own. Even when he took off his glove and groped for Johnny's pulse it was his own hammering heart he found.

Gradually, though, his training was taking over. He could not let Johnny continue to lie on his back, the worst possible position for a heart attack patient because it made the heart have to work so hard. Between the three of them, they managed to sit him upright. Nigel helped him get the resuscitation pack off his back so that he could give him some oxygen.

'He was convinced that if he tried to move he would be sucked off the side of the platform and that would be the end'

'He really was very sick
... The man was going
to die if he didn't do something'

But there were limits to what Steve could do. He would like to have had the electrocardiograph monitor that they carried on the ambulance, so he could see what Johnny's heart was doing. Its defibrillator could shock his heart back to life if it stopped. But there just was no way they could have carried it up. And, anyway, trying to administer electric jolts on that metal platform would probably give them all a shock big enough to throw them off.

The priority was to get him down to the ground as fast as they could. His condition was deteriorating and, lying there with the wind whistling around him, he was getting cold and running the risk of shock induced by hypothermia. He could go into a full cardiac arrest at any time and, when that happened, he would not stand a chance unless he was in the back of the ambulance or, better still, in hospital. The question was: how to do it?

Nigel Firkins had already ruled out using the fire service equipment. Nothing they had would reach. His first idea was to lower him down the inside of the crane tower, alongside the ladder. He had already called for a special stretcher with straps that would hold a casualty secure even if it was upright.

Steve didn't like the idea. His patient was getting worse by the minute, and it would take too long. Worse, it would mean a lot of stress for Johnny being lowered like that, and there was no way Steve could be with him to keep track of his condition. That plan would not work, but he couldn't think of one that would.

It was then that Patsy Mitchell came up with his own suggestion. He did not think they would get Johnny down by the ladder either; the stretcher would get caught and tossed about so much on the way down his friend would be dead before he reached the bottom.

He had been a crane driver a long time, and had often used the crane to lift injured people down from high buildings. Men were always breaking bones and needing to be lowered in some sort of container down to the ground.

A skip was the thing, he said. It would be quick, relatively gentle, and could put him down right next to the ambulance. The difficulty would be to get the skip up close enough to the bell platform to get the stretcher across and into it. He said he would drive the crane and organize the operation. He didn't like taking all that responsibility, but Johnny was his mate.

The others agreed. There did not seem to be any other way.

Patsy disappeared into the cab and got on the radio to the men down below. It was his idea, and he was determined it would work. The key to the operation was to get them to shorten the chains in which the skip was hanging as much as possible, so that he could get it right up close to the boom and right alongside the platform. He made them rig the chains again and again until he was satisfied they were as short as they could be, then he started the lift.

Now the crane was in operation it was even more difficult to work on the cramped platform. There was very little room for them to move anyway, the wind was whistling around them and dragging at their clothes, and now the whole structure started to flex and twist as the boom took up the load.

Nigel tried to concentrate on his immediate surroundings, and on encouraging Steve. He was grateful the ambulanceman was there, but he was obviously in a bad way and he wondered what would happen when they had to step off into space with the casualty to get into the skip. If he was shaky now, what would he be like then?

Steve had already had another panic attack. Nigel had told him the skip was on its way up and he had looked over to see where it was coming from. It was the first time he had taken a proper look down. The skip looked like a matchbox. The people really did look like ants, and the ambulance and fire engines smaller than toys. The skip got bigger and bigger as it seemed to rush towards him. He felt a sharp spasm of fear, and he thought he was going to be sick.

The skip arrived with another firefighter and the stretcher. Nigel and Steve buckled Johnny into the stretcher with trembling hands. Steve knew that he would have to get into the skip first, to pull Johnny across and be in a position to treat him if his condition suddenly deteriorated. But there was still quite a gap between the skip and the platform, and the wind was buffeting everything around. He was terrified before he had even started this operation. Now he was having to step off into mid-air, 180 feet off the ground. It's madness, he thought. Absolute madness.

He kept saying to Nigel, 'Hold on to me, hold on to me.' Nigel was doing his best, but he was also trying to keep hold of the skip at the same time as keeping up a stream of reassurance for Steve.

His teeth chattering with fear so much he could barely speak, Steve climbed over the bar on the side of the platform. It was, he thought, like bungy jumping without the bungy. It crossed his mind that it was only Nigel and the other firefighter's hands that were holding this huge, heavy skip alongside. One gust of wind at the wrong time and he would step into thin air.

He closed his eyes and jumped, caught his foot and fell headlong into the skip.

He stood up, trying to fight the fear. It felt just like a wobbly bin, swaying on the end of a string, and now they had to get the stretcher into it.

They had talked about how it would have to be done. How they would have to ease Johnny gently across so as to jolt him as little as possible. In the event, things turned out differently. They managed to get his head across, so that the stretcher bridged the gap between the skip and the crane. But the skip had really begun to sway around. The ropes and buckles under the stretcher were stopping it sliding smoothly across, and Johnny was a big man, a heavy weight to push.

Nigel was trying to hold it with one hand and push the stretcher with the other. Steve yelled, 'Shove! Shove like hell!' and yanked as hard as he could. The stretcher gave a lurch and jerked into the skip on top of Steve. Nigel slipped neatly over the side as well, and all four of them were safely inside.

That was not the end of the ordeal for Steve. He tried to concentrate on giving Johnny oxygen, but Patsy was intent on getting the skip down as fast as he could. He drove it out to the end of the boom at the same time as he turned the crane itself to bring the skip over the ambulance. Steve thought it felt like the devil's own fairground ride.

The bump when it hit the ground was the best feeling he had ever had. He was full of a kind of ecstasy. He couldn't talk, he just wanted to cry.

The best thing was that Johnny survived. Steve did not think he would, even when he was in the ambulance on the way to hospital. But there was something tough about Johnny O'Keefe, and he now looks like a man in the prime of health and life. 'God,' he says,

'There was still a gap between the skip and the platform, and the wind was buffeting everything around'

'must have had enough crane drivers that day.'

He is retired now, back in his native Ireland. If you talk to him about the day he had his heart attack he jokes about it. Especially the moment when the ambulanceman appeared on the platform, pale and rigid with fear.

'You'd have thought,' Johnny says, 'it was him that had had the heart attack. But that lad saved my life.'

Dealing with Fear of Heights

As many as 600,000 people suffer from an acute anxiety about heights, known medically as acrophobia. It's a condition that seriously disrupts their daily lives. Some people are too scared to walk down a flight of stairs, others won't have a first-floor office because they're afraid of throwing themselves out of a window. Most of the time people with that kind of fear simply avoid high places – they keep away from bridges and cliffs and highrise buildings. But in an emergency, they might have to climb down a fire escape. How many of us would understand what they're going through?

Vertigo

They may be suffering from vertigo, dizziness that literally throws their world into a spin. Their fear may result in a distortion of their world. Buildings and steps appear twice their actual size, or seem to lean towards them. Their anxiety may make them breathe too fast, they may feel sick and disorientated. You don't have to be an expert to help. There are a few simple things you can do.

1 CALM THEM DOWN. Help them to breathe slowly and evenly.

2 TALK TO THEM about general things. Help to distract them from their fear until they're in control. Never say 'pull yourself together'.

3 Give CALM, CLEAR INSTRUCTIONS. Never shout. Help them down one step at a time.

4 KEEP THEM MOVING slowly and steadily – don't let them stop, they may freeze up completely.

5 When safely on the ground LAY THEM DOWN to reduce the dizziness if necessary and praise them for their achievement.

If you suffer from acrophobia you can get professional help through the National Health Service. Ask your doctor to put you in touch with someone who can talk you through your fear. There are counsellors all over the country as well as self-help groups like Triumph over Phobia and First Steps to Freedom. Slowly but surely you can gain in confidence and overcome your fear.

Advice is obtainable from:

First Steps to Freedom
22 Randall Road
Kenilworth
Warwickshire CV8 1JY
tel. 0926-851608

PAX
4 Manorbrook
Blackheath
London SE3 9AW
tel. 081-318 5026
(Free booklet and membership application form available)

Phobic Action: a national charity with a helpline you can call on 081-559 2459.

Triumph over Phobia (TOP UK)
Mrs J. Bonham Christie
4 Marlborough Buildings
Bath BA1 2LX
tel. 0225-314129
(Send £1.50 for information pack)

In addition there are several useful books on the subject available from good bookshops.

Dealing with a Heart Attack

Every year 100,000 people die of a heart attack in the UK, but as many as 10,000 lives could be saved if more people recognized the early warning signs and called for help quickly.

What is a heart attack?

An attack happens when the blood supply to the heart muscle is suddenly reduced, for example when there's a blockage or clot in one of the arteries carrying blood to the heart. This can happen to anyone – you don't have to have a previous history of heart disease.

Heart attacks vary in severity. The effect depends largely on how much of the heart muscle is affected. Not all heart attack victims will collapse and many make a complete recovery. Heart attacks are not always life-threatening, but it is important to recognize the warning signs. The majority of patients who die from attacks do so within the first two hours of the onset of symptoms. The most obvious symptom is a pain in the centre of the chest which just doesn't go away. The type of pain may vary. It may feel like severe indigestion or a band being gradually tightened. It doesn't start suddenly, but builds up slowly over a period of minutes.

Occasionally, a heart attack may occur with the victim experiencing only minor feelings of discomfort, like breathlessness, nausea, sweating and faintness.

Warning signs of a heart attack

- persistent crushing pain in centre of chest
- shortness of breath
- feeling sick
- feeling dizzy
- sweating
- ashen skin and blue lips
- irregular pulse

If you recognize someone is having a heart attack, the first thing to do is get help. If you can, send someone else to phone for an ambulance, but make sure they explain that it's a suspected heart attack and always ask them to come back and tell you that help is on its way.

What you should do

Make the person comfortable – keep them warm, loosen any tight clothing and try to help them to sit up. A half-sitting position with head and shoulders supported and knees bent is often the most comfortable and should help to reduce the work of the heart.

If they are conscious don't be tempted to give them anything to eat or drink, not even water. But if you have an aspirin, offer this to them and let them chew it slowly. It helps by thinning the blood and preventing clots from forming. But be aware that some people are allergic to aspirin so it would be dangerous for them to take it. Offer one only in circumstances where you know the medical history of the person involved and where you are sure they don't have a history of internal bleeding. If in doubt, don't take any risks – wait until the emergency services and a doctor arrive.

The main risk during any heart attack is that the casualty will suffer a cardiac arrest. This is when the heart suddenly stops beating. If this happens, both the breathing and pulse will stop, so watch the casualty all the time, and if they lose consciousness, be ready to carry out the ABC of resuscitation:

AIRWAY – Open the airway

BREATHING – Check for breathing

CIRCULATION – Check the pulse

If the casualty *is* breathing and *does* have a pulse, put them in the recovery position. If the casualty is *not* breathing but *does* have a pulse, start mouth-to-mouth breathing for them.

If the casualty is *not* breathing and does *not* have a pulse, call for an ambulance immediately and then start mouth-to-mouth breathing and chest compressions. (See also pages 69–70)

If you don't know how to carry out the ABC of resuscitation, learn it on a first-aid course. You'll then be able to keep the casualty's brain supplied with oxygen until the ambulance arrives, and so increase the chances of survival.

The ambulance will be equipped with a special machine called a defibrillator. This is used to monitor all suspected heart attack victims, and it may be used to start the heart beating normally with an electric shock. This can be quite a disturbing sight, particularly if it's happening to someone you know.

Remember, your prompt action can mean the difference between life and death.

CHAPTER 7

Tidal Rock

They were full of enthusiasm that January. They did not mind the cold, or the long hike to where the boat was parked, out by the railway line in the middle of nowhere. It was hard work. They did some structural repairs on the hull and wheelhouse. They gave it a coat of paint, and did their best to service the big old diesel engine. It was an improvement, but a bit short of a complete overhaul. Nevertheless, after three weeks they felt they were ready.

Left to right) Allan MacIntyre, Peter Gramalis and Ian MacIntyre meet in Oban for the reconstruction

It was called *The Golden West*, and that was where they were taking it. Up to the tourist towns of Scotland's west coast to make them maybe not a fortune, but at least a living.

It had looked far from golden when Ian MacIntyre had first seen it. Just an old fishing boat, a coastal crabber, decrepit, decommissioned and down at heel. It was a sad sight, washed up there in a Glasgow backwater. But to Ian MacIntyre it was the future. It meant a fresh start after the years working on the North Sea oil rigs and drifting from job to job. For a couple of weeks he poked around it. He brought his friends to see it. He weighed it all up and eventually made his decision.

He paid around £2,500 to become *The Golden West*'s new owner. It had been a lot of money for him to raise, but it would be worth it if his plan worked out. The boat had been built to fish for crabs around the sea lochs of the jagged Scottish coastline. But that was a hard life, and an uncertain one. Ian MacIntyre wanted to use it to fish for tourists, up there in the crowded summer holiday towns of Fort William and Oban; take them out on fishing parties and sightseeing trips. The way he saw it, it could be a new life where the boat would make him and his friends money.

There were four of them on board, as the pilot pointed *The Golden West* out into the Clyde: Ian MacIntyre and his younger brother Allan, together with two friends of Ian's from his days in primary school, thirty or more years before. Robert 'Rab' Quigley had been in the same class, Peter Gramalis was a couple of years older. They had all done a bit of this, a bit of that, in their lives. Now they were all keen to try something new.

They spent the first night at Gourock, where the wide river turns abruptly south and broadens out into the Firth of Clyde. The next day they headed west, across the Firth, and then north into the sheltered channel between the Isle of Bute and the mainland, before anchoring at Port Driseach. They had picked a route that kept them well away from the open sea and there had been no real problems. The hull was letting in some water, but the pump that was driven by the diesel engine was more than able to cope. The weather was fine, their spirits were high, everything was going to plan.

Their luck held the next day as they motored round Ardlamont Point and up Loch Fyne to Lochgilphead, the start of the Crinan Canal that slices through the great long finger of Knapdale to the open sea, and cuts days off the journey to the north-west.

When the fourth day dawned they were at the western end of the canal. It was, they thought, a simple four- or five-hour trip to Oban, their next stop.

The boat was going well. They were still in high spirits. They were nearly there. In the event, it was to be the longest day of their lives; very nearly the *last* day of their lives.

The lock-keeper opened the final lock at half-past ten that morning to let *The Golden West* and its scratch crew into the sea loch that led out to the islands. It was later than they had hoped, but the weather was clear and they still had plenty of time to complete their journey before dark. It was fine enough for Ian MacIntyre to decide to head for the Strait of Corryvreckan, a narrow and, in bad weather, dangerous strip of water between the islands of Jura and Scarba. There were rocks, sandbanks, even a whirlpool on its northern side, but *The Golden West* sailed serenely past all the hazards and safely out into the Firth of Lorn.

These waters, where the prevailing winds and the tidal streams funnel down from the open sea through to the narrow straits between Mull and the mainland, are known to sailors as the Great Race. For the first time since the four men had left Glasgow the wind started to blow up and the seas began to get rough. It was nothing too daunting for men who had worked the rigs in the North Sea, force four at the most. But the swell made it uncomfortable, and it was bitterly cold. The temperature was down to $-3\,°C$, and the wind pushed the chill factor much lower. After an hour and a half, the wind began to die down as they got up into the more sheltered part of the Firth.

They began to recover their high spirits. But that was the moment when it all started to go wrong.

It was Peter Gramalis who had noticed it first. He had been brought along because he had been to sea a few times in merchant ships and knew a bit about diesel engines. He knew what was happening when he saw oil flying out of the exhaust pipe and heard the engine starting to falter. He knew, but there wasn't anything he could do about it. He yelled up to Ian in the wheelhouse and, together, they poked around in the diesel's insides. One look told Peter what he knew already; salt water had got into the engine and the oil was

'The boat was going well. They were still in high spirits. They were nearly there. In the event it was to be the longest day of their lives; very nearly the *last* day of their lives'

emulsifying and coagulating in the gearbox.

It did not seem too bad at first. They were not much more than an hour from Oban and for a time they were able to keep the engine going in the one gear. But, a few minutes later, Peter shouted up again. The engine began to seize up completely. It stopped once, and they managed to get it started again. Then it stopped for good.

They had some tools on board, but Ian was convinced the gasket had gone, and they did not have a replacement. Worse, the water was rising in the bottom of the boat. The main pump had been able to keep up with the leaks in the hull. But it was powered by the engine, and when the engine stopped, the pump stopped. *The Golden West* was starting to sink.

They had a spare electric pump, but that proved useless. For every gallon it pumped out of the bilges, ten more came in. They tried to bail the water out by hand, but they soon realized they hadn't a hope of keeping pace with the rate the water was flooding in. There was nothing they could do for themselves; they had to call for help.

The problem was, they had no means of doing so.

They had taken a few risks when they had cast off in *The Golden West* and headed out to sea. It had no lights, but they had thought that would not matter because they were not intending to sail at night. They had no lifeboat or dinghy. Worse, they had no radio. It was not strictly illegal to sail without one, and they were planning to have one fitted when they got to Fort William. They were taking a chance, and they had been caught out.

Even at this time of year, there were boats plying up and down the Firth, out of Oban, to and from the islands. They somehow had to attract attention, and fast. Darkness wasn't far away and time was running out. The water was now thigh-deep down below. Peter and Rab were huddled, speechless, in the wheelhouse and Allan was starting to panic. Ian remembered there were some distress flares in the front hold, and brought them up on deck.

The two big parachute flares turned out to be duds. The two hand-held flares did work after a short struggle, so Ian and Allan stood, waving them from the stern of the boat until they fizzled out, and the brightness faded away into the winter's gloaming.

They were resourceful men and did not give up. One of them suggested lighting a fire on deck. Between them, they manhandled a paint drum up from the hold, filled it with diesel and set light to it. There was still just enough daylight for smoke to be seen, so they threw a tyre on to the flames, then the dud flares, and finally everything combustible they could lay their hands on.

Surely *somebody* would see them.

But nobody did, and all the time *The Golden West* was filling up with water, sinking slowly beneath their feet.

Common sense told them they had to get nearer the shore if they were to stand any chance. Instinct made them rig up a temporary sail, a tarpaulin stretched from the bow to wheelhouse, that caught the north-westerly breeze and pushed the now-waterlogged *Golden West* sluggishly towards the rocks.

The grey dusk turned quickly into the absolute black of the northern night; the temperature went on falling. The fire in the paint drum was still roaring away and they huddled round that. They were cold and frightened. Their fire was starting to burn a hole in the deck. They wondered whether the flames would reach the two 45-gallon drums of diesel before the boat sank; whether they would be blown up or drown in the freezing water.

Ian still thought they might drift on to a beach; just a chance they might be saved and the boat salvaged. But the others thought they were finished.

They were very quiet but, then, they had a lot to be quiet about.

They could not see it in the dark, but the wind eventually pushed the sinking boat to within half a mile of the shore. The first they knew was when the bottom scraped against a ridge of rock and *The Golden West* started to grind back and forth with the rise and fall of the waves. Each movement wrenched open the seams of the hull still wider and it was obvious to all of them that the boat was going to go down.

Ian and Rab had done survival training in their time on the rigs. They had had lectures about hypothermia and they urged the other two to put on all the clothes they could find, and the lifejackets on top, because it was inevitable now that they were going to end up in the freezing water.

Ian had noticed how quiet Peter was, sitting alone aft, not saying a word. He didn't seem to want to try to save himself, and the others couldn't understand what was the matter with him. Even though they had known him all those years, there was one thing about him

'Surely *somebody* would see them. But nobody did, and all the time *The Golden West* was filling up with water, sinking slowly beneath their feet' they did not know. Something that was vitally important now.

He couldn't swim.

In any case, he told them when he had confessed his secret, it wouldn't make any difference. The water was so cold your heart would stop as soon as you jumped in; the sea would get you either way. They shuffled up to the bow of the boat and waited for the ship to sink.

It did not take long. *The Golden West* was breaking up fast. From where they were they could just see the stern settling down into the water. Then the water swept up the deck and filled the wheelhouse. Allan had been further back than the other three but now he ran forward to join them, shouting, 'We're going now.'

They linked hands as the boat reared. The bow lifted straight out of the water, and *The Golden West* slid with a whooshing noise, stern first, to the bottom. They waited until the water was up to their knees and stepped off together.

God, it was cold. Peter was surprised it hadn't given him an instant heart attack, the shock seemed intense enough. The others felt the same as they struggled in the wash left by the sinking boat.

They had lost contact with each other as soon as they had gone into the water. Rab and Ian came to the surface at the same time and struck out for a rock they could see a dozen or so yards away. Allan surfaced a second or two later and followed them. The three clambered on to the rock and looked around, but there was no sign of Peter.

They shouted and screamed in the darkness, but there was no reply. Then Ian spotted his body floating a few yards away. They watched it as it drifted past them with no sign of movement, and they thought he was dead. Then, when the body reached the next rock along from them, they saw his hand move out and cling on to it. They cheered as they watched him pull himself out of the water, and went back in themselves to swim across to him.

The four friends were reunited; alive, for the moment, but in the most perilous of situations. Nobody knew what had happened to them. Nobody knew they were lost. They were stuck on a bare and remote rock in the Sound of Insh. They did not know precisely where they were, or how far they were from the shore. They were already wet through and cold, and they faced a long, midwinter night with the temperature already several degrees below freezing.

Any objective assessment of their chances would have put them at near zero, even without one final twist of fate.

The rock they had chosen was what seamen call a tidal rock. At high tide it was often completely under water.

And the tide was rising.

They did not realize it for quite some time. They were preoccupied with their own thoughts, and with finding a place on the rock that would give them even a tiny bit of shelter.

Ian was coming to terms with the idea that he had lost a lot of money; *The Golden West* had represented a big slice of his savings and it was not insured. He did not dwell on that for very long. After all, he kept telling himself, he might lose his life as well before the night was out, and so might his friends.

It was his boat; his idea. He felt responsible for what had happened to them all, and it was not a nice feeling.

Allan could see the blurred outline of what he thought was the shore across a channel, only a few hundred yards away. He was all for swimming for it, there and then. But his brother told him he was a fool. He could not see where he was going; there would be currents and tides that would sweep him off into the night and he would never be seen again. Best to wait until dawn. Allan let himself be persuaded.

The four of them looked for a place to settle down for the night. The rock was bare, worn smooth by a million waves. There was no shelter anywhere against the wind and spray, but they did find a small dip in the contour of the rock, an indentation in its surface, just enough to hold a puddle of seawater.

They lay down there in the freezing cold darkness. They cuddled together to try to conserve what little warmth they had, and told each other through chattering teeth they had to keep awake. To sleep would be to die.

Gradually, they began to realize that the tide was rising up the rock. The spray, which had only scattered a few drops over them when they first crawled on to it, was now drenching them with every other wave. When one of them felt seaweed on one of the highest points on the rock they knew for certain what they had already begun to suspect. The place they had chosen as a refuge was often totally under water.

They were not religious men, but they prayed. To the One God, and any other that might be listening. There wasn't much else they could do.

> 'Gradually, they began to realize that the tide was rising up the rock. The spray, which had only scattered a few drops over them when they first crawled on to it, was now drenching them with every other wave'

They had been on the rock about three hours, and the tide had risen to within a few feet of them, when it seemed all their prayers had been answered.

A dull thudding over the dark horizon to the north became a louder and louder clatter, a jumble of lights, and finally the great bulk of a rescue helicopter that roared right over them.

They stood up, they waved, they yelled until they were hoarse, but the helicopter showed no sign of seeing them. It held course, steadily, to the south. In a few moments the lights had disappeared, then the noise died away, and they were left with the sea and the night.

At least, they said to each other as they tried to cope with the disappointment, it proved that people were looking for them. Somebody had reported them missing. The search was on and if only they could survive the night they were bound to be found.

They were not to know they were wrong.

The helicopter wasn't looking for them. Nobody knew about them at all.

The men on the Oban lifeboat stamped about on the deck, as it hugged the coast and played its searchlight over the patchwork of rocks. They had been out since six o'clock that evening, and despite all their layers of warm clothing, despite the hot soup from the tiny lifeboat galley, they were bitterly cold. Ice was building up on the deck. It was the coldest night of the winter. God only knew what the men they were looking for were feeling. If they were still alive, of course.

It was yet another twist in an extraordinary story. Two boats had got into trouble that day in the waters between the Isle of Mull and the mainland. Two crews had escaped when their boats had foundered and were stranded on rocks, waiting to be rescued. But the searchers did not know that. As far as they were concerned, only one was missing.

They had been called out shortly after dark. A small boat called *The Three Sisters* was overdue at Oban. It, and the two men on board, were reported missing. The rescue helicopter was scrambled. The Tobermory lifeboat took up station in the Firth of Lorn, maintaining a radar watch, in case the boat was still afloat and drifting, while the Oban lifeboat searched the shoreline.

You had to be very lucky to find somebody at night, the lifeboat coxswain, Pat McLean, thought, not for the first time. The coast was so rugged, so peppered with rocks, that it was difficult to get in close. The searchlight played across the shore, but it was hard to make out what was there. There were patches of different colours, lots of debris. You think you have found something and it turns out to be an old fishbox. His crew carried on, and tried to keep warm. They knew the search would soon be called off.

Sure enough, just before midnight the coastguard told them to go home.

On the rock, the crew of *The Golden West* were struggling to keep awake, fighting hard to stay alive. The waves had lapped up close to them. The spray had drenched them over and over again. But when they thought they might have to swim for it, the water had begun to recede. By sheer luck they had foundered on one of the lowest tides of the year.

'On the rock, the crew of *The Golden West* were struggling to keep awake, fighting hard to stay alive'

They didn't feel lucky. They were colder than they had ever been in their lives. They had stopped shivering, which Ian knew was a danger sign for hypothermia. Strangely, his teeth were still chattering, which made it difficult to talk, difficult to keep the others awake. Their legs and arms were going numb. When they tried to move they felt pins and needles all over their bodies.

Allan was restless. He seemed to be the only one with any energy. He was trying to keep warm by constant movement but it wasn't working. It felt as if his blood had turned to ice. He wished he had swum for the shore as soon as the boat went down, and wondered if he would still have the strength when daylight came; whether he would still be alive, for that matter.

Peter was very quiet, but then he always was. His mind was wandering, as he lay on his back looking at the hills and the stars. The stars seemed to form weird and wonderful patterns of their own. Sometimes he could even forget about the cold. It was like going to the movies. If you could sell an experience like that people would go out and buy it.

Apart from the fact it might be the last thing you ever experienced, he thought, as he started to drift off to sleep and was woken by a nudge from Rab.

The Oban lifeboat set out again before dawn to resume the search. It was heading straight for the rock where the men from *The Golden West* were still struggling to stay alive. In the growing daylight they couldn't have failed to see them, and found four men, rather than the two they were searching for. But fate, which had played with those men all along, pulled another trick.

The lifeboat was only twenty minutes away from them when a radio message from the coastguard called the search off. A fishing boat called *The Golden Opportunity* had found the two men from *The Three Sisters* still alive on an island covered with heather a few miles to the north. The lifeboat was ordered to turn round and pick them up. Once they had dropped them back at Oban, they were under orders to take part in a routine exercise that was already planned for that morning. The emergency was over.

As dawn broke over their rock, Allan MacIntyre was weighing his chances of swimming across to the mainland. At low tide it looked no more than a hundred yards across, but it was difficult to tell whether there were any tidal riffs or currents that would pull him out into the main channel and drown him. His brother still felt it was better to sit tight, and wait for the rescue he kept telling the others was inevitable. Allan did not believe it and, in his heart, neither did Ian.

Allan paced up and down a few times, trying to psych himself up. It was up to him, he thought. He was the youngest. He was the best swimmer. All the others had children.

He couldn't stand it on the rock any longer. Anyway, if he did not go then, he would soon be too weak to try.

As he debated with himself, and argued with the others, he saw something which made up his mind in a flash: smoke, rising from behind a saddle in the low hills on the shore. Smoke from a chimney. People, warmth, safety. He slipped down into the water and set off for the shore.

The cold struck deep into him. The currents tried to pull him out of the channel, and his clothes seemed to weigh a ton. He was a good swimmer, but it was so difficult to move. The front of the lifejacket kept banging into his face as the force of the water pushed it back over his head. He kept turning over, swimming for a few moments on his front, then rolling on to his back and pushing himself on with just his legs. Swim, kick, swim. Swim, kick, swim.

He didn't know how long it was before his feet felt the bottom again. He pulled himself on to the shore, exhausted but triumphant, and worked his way up to the top of a low ridge to see where the smoke was coming from.

It was the worst moment of his life. Before him was another stretch of water. He had not reached the mainland, he was on another island. He would have to do it all again.

For a moment he thought he couldn't do it. But he could still see the smoke, curling up behind the hill, with its promise of warmth and safety. He gathered himself and walked down into the water again.

It was the same nightmare struggle. The same current trying to drag him away. The same wearying process. Swim, kick, swim.

An age passed, and then he reached the shore. There was no sense of triumph this time; all he wanted to do was lie down in the mud and go to sleep.

From the rock his friends could see him as he tried to stand up, and wondered if he would ever be able to climb the hill. From that distance, he looked on the point of collapse, weaving and staggering up from the shoreline like a Saturday-night drunk.

Allan's reserves of strength were all but gone. It was only the smoke that, somehow, drew him up the hill. When he reached the top of the saddle in the ridge he could see a pub and some houses. He fell down the hill towards them. If it hadn't have been downhill then he would have been finished.

Lars Brunner, the teenage son of the publican, was clearing up in the front bar when the door crashed open and a strange man with sodden clothes and face covered in oil stood swaying and trying desperately to speak to him. The words would not come out. All he could manage was: 'There are others.'

Lars called his mother, Miranda. She thought for a moment the man had fallen off the back of a coal lorry, he was so filthy. It was a quiet place in the winter, and his appearance was a shock. But she quickly realized he was in a bad way.

Miranda pushed him close to the fire and stripped away his

'He pulled himself on to the shore, exhausted but triumphant'

sodden clothes. She wrapped him in warm blankets. It was several minutes before he managed to stutter out what had happened to him and tell them the other three were still out on the rock.

A few minutes later, the Oban lifeboat had its second emergency call in two days. It broke away from the exercise and once more headed south along the coast. The lifeboatmen couldn't believe there was another crew lost and stranded there. It was getting to be a trend.

It took another half an hour before the lifeboat reached the rock. By now the three men were in a bad way. Their memories were starting to go; they were beginning to hallucinate. But when they saw the lifeboat chugging towards them they stood up and jumped around as if they were mad.

Miranda Brunner 'quickly realized that he was in a bad way'

There were too many rocks for the lifeboat to come in and pick them up; they were ferried over in a rubber dinghy. The lifeboatmen took them below, wrapped them in thermal blankets and gave them tea and Mars bars. They were drowsy and fuddled, but alive. Halfway back to Oban they started shivering again, which showed they had begun to recover from the hypothermia. An ambulance was waiting at the dockside to take them to hospital, and they were kept there, under observation, that day and overnight. After all they had been through, they thought it was the most comfortable place they had ever known.

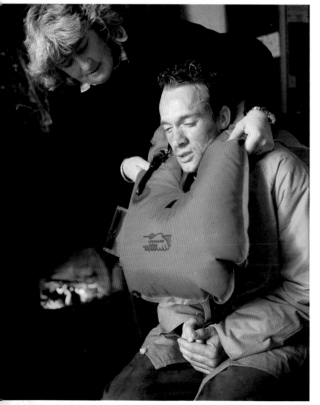

The Brunners were kind to them, washing Allan's clothes and bringing a bottle of wine to the hospital. The following day, when they were discharged, the four men went down to the pub to repay the hospitality. A friendship that continues.

And the great plan did not die with *The Golden West*. They have bought another boat, and they are doing it up to go and fish for tourists up on the west coast.

This time, they say, they'll do one or two things differently. . .

Hypothermia

Swimming in cold water is a classic cause of accidental hypothermia. It's believed that many deaths attributed in the past to drowning are in fact due to hypothermia – cold shock. For most months of the year the sea, rivers and lakes of the UK are cold enough to cause rapid cooling of the body. Allan MacIntyre suffered from hypothermia in very unusual circumstances, but people of all ages may develop it following prolonged exposure to extremely cold weather: for example, trapped in a broken-down car in snow, or sheltering on a mountainside after an accident. Knowing how to prevent or treat someone suffering from hypothermia could save a life.

Who is most vulnerable?

Hypothermia is when the body temperature falls below 35°C. Three groups of people are most vulnerable: the elderly living in poorly heated homes, because as the body ages it gradually loses its sensitivity to cold; babies sleeping in cold bedrooms, because they lose heat rapidly and cannot easily reverse a fall in temperature, and those involved in outdoor sports, especially mountaineers, cavers and swimmers.

Signs of hypothermia

There are several early warning signs that someone is in trouble. They lose control of their movement and start stumbling, and their speech is often slurred. They suffer from intense shivering and may exhibit completely irrational behaviour. An example of this is

'mountain disrobing syndrome' – when people feel compelled to rip off their clothes, even though they're in freezing conditions.

Someone suffering from hypothermia will feel unnaturally cold to the touch, rather like marble, particularly if you put your hand on their abdomen or under their armpit. In severe hypothermia, breathing becomes slow and shallow, and the heart may beat only faintly or irregularly. Eventually the intense shivering stops and the person becomes unconscious. Babies suffering from hypothermia have misleadingly pink faces, hands and feet, but their skin feels intensely cold and they are drowsy and limp.

How to avoid hypothermia

If you go walking or climbing in cold weather always make sure you are well equipped. Remember, you are vulnerable to hypothermia if you have an accident or become lost.

● Take plenty of extra warm and waterproof clothing.

● Carry a survival bag lined with space blankets into which you can crawl to wait for help.

● Take some food and flasks of warm drinks.

● Tell someone where you are going, what you are doing and when you will be back.

How can you help?

● If you suspect someone is suffering from hypothermia, always seek immediate medical attention.

● In mild cases, where someone is conscious, warm them up slowly. Warm sugary drinks, like tea, will help. Don't give them really hot drinks, hot water bottles or hot baths – these may make them collapse.

● Never give them alcohol and never try and give an unconscious person anything to eat or drink.

● Make sure the head is covered – a quarter of our body heat is lost through the head.

● In more severe cases, lay them down flat, call an ambulance and get them to hospital as soon as possible.

● If you're out in the open you must keep them warm and stay warm yourself. Find shelter, and provide protection from the wind and rain by using a polythene cover.

● Insulate them from the cold with dry blankets or a sleeping bag.

● If they stop shivering don't assume they're recovering. Their temperature may have dropped too low for body-warming mechanisms to function.

● If you can't find a pulse, don't assume they're dead. The body temporarily shuts down in extreme cold to conserve energy. It has been known for hypothermic casualties to survive when their body temperature has fallen as low as 20°C.

● In very severe cases of hypothermia, victims may be admitted to an intensive care unit for controlled warming.

CHAPTER 8

Where the Buck Stops

The men and women who come when you call 999 can't turn the job down if they don't like the look of it. They can't say, 'Sorry, we didn't do this on the training course. You'd better get somebody else.' They are called because there *is* nobody else. They are the bottom line on wheels. Where the buck stops.

That was why paramedic Steve Mortley did what he did that evening in June. They could all see the casualty lying, face down, in his own back garden. He was badly hurt and quite possibly dying. But they could also see what was trying to kill him and they all knew that to go near would mean risking the same fate. Someone had to try, and Steve knew it had to be him. Besides, he kept telling himself, bees are not aggressive creatures.

999 'He kept telling himself, bees are not aggressive creatures'

Bees are older than man. They have been found perfectly preserved in amber from thirty million years ago. There is evidence that cavemen plundered honey from their nests. Modern man relies on them to pollinate his crops and his gardens. He farms them because he still likes honey, even though he can now buy a thousand cheaper forms of sweetness. He admires the bees that make it for their industry and their selflessness. He sees 75,000 individuals all working until they drop for the good of the hive.

For thousands of years he has been able to manage bees, but never tame them. They are still wild animals, driven by instincts he can only partly understand.

Sometimes that instinct is to kill.

It had been a beautiful midsummer day. It was still hot in the early evening as Peter Gregory carried a pile of washing over to the clothesline near the fence of his back garden at Wymondham in Norfolk. His son, Michael, was playing in the garden. Their lodger, Ross Wallace, was sitting out drinking a cup of coffee and trying, yet again, to finish off the crossword in the paper. Next door, out of sight beyond the fence, their 78-year-old neighbour was tending his beehives. All in all, a peaceful summer's evening in a quiet country town.

A waving arm crossed the corner of Ross's eye. He looked up to see Peter flailing about by the washing line, but he had just solved one of the clues in his crossword and wanted to write it in. When he next glanced up Peter was thrashing at himself, and running in small circles. The words 'whirling dervish' came into Ross's mind. He didn't quite know what that was, but he was sure Peter looked like one. It was only a momentary thought because it was obvious something was seriously wrong.

Peter started screaming and his movements became more frantic. Ross wondered if he was having an epileptic fit. He got out of his chair to go and help him.

It had only taken a few seconds. The noise first, a terrible roaring sound in Peter's ears. Then a sting – *zap* in the back of the neck. The shock of it had barely sunk in before there were more. *Zap, zap, zap.* He knew almost at once the bees were out to get him and tried to swat at them and brush them off, but they were everywhere. He tried to run away, but couldn't see where he was going. He screamed for help. They were stinging every bit of his body they could reach by now. At all costs he had to keep them out of his eyes, his nose and his mouth, but he couldn't cover them all with his hands.

As a last resort he threw himself on to the ground and tried to bury his face in the grass. The bees gathered in a mass on his head and shoulders. The roaring in his ears became unbearable, and he passed out.

Ross didn't see the bees until he got close to Peter's body. At first, it looked as though there was a cloth over his head and shoulders. But, as he got nearer, the cloth turned into a writhing clump of bees. The noise was extraordinary; the bees seemed to sizzle with fury. There was something scary about them, almost evil. It was clear to Ross that Peter would not be able to stand that kind of attack for long. Unless someone got the bees off him, he would die. The question was, how?

He ran indoors and fetched a tea towel. It was an instinctive decision, and a wrong one. He lashed at the bees and only made them more agitated. Some started to attack him, and followed him as he was forced to run for cover back into the house.

His next attempt was even worse. He brought out a bucket of water and threw it over Peter's head and neck. It did nothing, except make the bees more angry still. They were finding their way into Ross's hair by now, and stinging him. He couldn't think of what else he could do for Peter and was worried about Michael, who was still standing on the edge of the lawn in a state of shock. He pushed him inside the house and closed the patio doors behind them.

Between them they closed all the windows. It was a hard thing for Ross to do, difficult to justify to himself then, and since. They were safe inside the house. But, just outside the window, Peter had begun squirming on the ground and screaming; he might well be dying in front of their eyes.

Given that they did not know what to do, it was the right decision. Left alone the bees might have gone away of their own accord. They were only risking themselves, and if the bees had turned on Michael he would have been in serious danger. An attack of that ferocity on a child of twelve would almost certainly have proved fatal.

Ross tried to keep him away from the window so he couldn't

see what was happening to his dad, and wondered whom he could call for help. The beekeeper next door was the obvious choice, but his hearing was poor and he was an elderly man. It wasn't worth the risk.

It always happens at the worst possible time. The lock on the front door of the bungalow had been playing up for months. But it wasn't until the day they had a desperate emergency that it froze up completely, trapping them inside. There was no phone in the house – Peter didn't like the idea of the office being able to get hold

(Above) 'It was still hot in the early evening' as Peter Gregory put his washing on the clothesline. (Insert) 'The roaring in his ears became unbearable, and he passed out'

of him – so they needed to get to a neighbour to call for an ambulance. They wrestled with the lock for several minutes before they realized they weren't going to shift it. Eventually, Michael managed to climb out of one of the bedroom windows, and raced off down the street.

Left to himself, Ross paced up and down by the window feeling helpless – and hopeless. It seemed unreal, like a bad dream or a horror film. A memory surfaced in his mind and it was frighteningly clear to him. It had been a report on 999 about a jogger who'd been stung while he was running along a towpath, and the big rescue operation that had only just saved his life. What worried him again and again as he stood by the window was that the jogger had only been stung *once*.

Outside, Peter was covered with hundreds of bees. He had gone still.

Ross was convinced he was dead.

Michael was back within a few minutes. He had called for an ambulance from a house across the road. Ross tried to work out how long it would take to come; half an hour, he thought. It's bound to be too late.

He sent Michael out again to the pub up the road. There might be somebody there who could do something. Anyway, it meant Michael wouldn't have to watch his father die.

Joe Gagick, landlord of the Green Dragon, knew a little about bees and a lot about the Gregorys. Peter was a regular, and Michael often came round to play with his kids. The boy was in a bad way when he came into the bar that evening, crying and not very coherent. His desperation and panic were obvious but he managed to get across that his father was in a bad way, and why.

Joe's father had kept bees himself, and the one thing he remembered was that they could be controlled with smoke. They had had a barbecue in the garden the night before and the can of diesel he had used to start the fire was still out there. He grabbed it and – for no obvious reason – picked up a garden rake as well. Two of his customers volunteered to help and together they ran round to the bungalow.

They found Peter unconscious, lying in the back garden. Joe managed to get quite close to him for a moment or two. The sight is still vivid in his memory. There was a thick, moving mat of bees all over his head and neck. They stretched down his back, and along the backs of his legs. There were hundreds and hundreds of them. He could see where they had stung him, and see the remains of the stings hanging off many of the insects that were crawling about. Many had got into Peter's ears, which made Joe shudder. He had never seen bees so wild or so angry.

He only had a few seconds before the bees turned their attention to him. He got the impression more and more were pouring over the fence, intent on attacking everything in sight.

He and his two regulars withdrew to the other side of the garden and set about lighting a fire to create enough smoke to drive the bees away. They found a couple of old potato sacks and poured diesel on to them. When they had got those well ablaze they covered them with grass cuttings left from when Peter had cut the lawn earlier in the day. The fire made just the right thick acrid smoke.

There was only one problem. The wind blew it in the wrong direction. The idea was good, the execution hopeless. Another rescue attempt had failed.

The call came through on the emergency phone, the direct link to ambulance control. It was clipped, to the point, the way they always are. A man had been stung by bees in Wymondham. It wasn't the normal kind of call but, then, it would be difficult to define what 'normal' is for a paramedic.

It was only a ten-minute drive from the ambulance base station at Attleborough to Wymondham. On the way the crew, Steve Mortley and Dave Money, tried to work out the possibilities, to prepare themselves for what they might find. They decided the most likely thing was a straightforward bee sting; somebody had panicked and called them out, and by now everybody would be a bit embarrassed when they turned up because he didn't need any treatment at all. It often happened.

Ambulance control had said the man might be unconscious. He might have been stung in the throat, causing a swelling that was blocking his airway.

The worst they could think of was a sting that had caused a severe allergic reaction, a rare condition known as anaphylactic shock. The very few people who are susceptible to it don't have that reaction

'There was a thick, moving mat of bees all over his head and neck . . . there were hundreds and hundreds of them'

the first time they are stung; it requires several stings to sensitize their bodies. Most people affected know that a sting means trouble, and carry the medication to counteract it. Nonetheless, someone in anaphylactic shock could be in real danger. Steve pressed harder on the accelerator.

Dave Money recognized the house when they arrived, and realized he knew the people involved. It was always an unsettling feeling; casualties are normally strangers.

He was first out of the ambulance. He snatched up the emergency case and ran down the side of the bungalow. He recognized Ross Wallace. He was standing in the window, pointing urgently to the back of the house and the garden.

When he got to the corner of the building he could see Peter lying, face down, in the grass. Even from there he could see the air above his body was thick with bees. He took a step forward and called out to him, but there was no response. He went a few more steps and called again. Now he could see bees around Peter's head and more of them swarming over his body. It looked for all the world like a scene from a Hitchcock movie, he thought.

At that moment, the bees turned on him. He was wearing a short-sleeved shirt. The bees were already on his arms and in his hair. It was no time for heroics. He turned and ran.

Steve was sorting out equipment at the back of the ambulance when Dave came rushing up to him, waving his hands above his head, and flicking bees off his body. They were both unprepared for the situation. The scenarios they had worked out all involved a single bee sting – not several hundred furious bees, intent on attacking everybody that crossed their path.

People were looking to them. Steve had noticed before how people tend to stop everything when the ambulance arrives. The neighbours had rushed up to tell them what was happening but were now keeping out of the way; the lodger and the son were back in the bungalow, and the three men from the pub were staying in the far corner of the garden with their useless fire. They were on their own.

They decided to split up. Dave went to look for the beekeeper, and Steve went to take a look at the patient for himself.

He yelled at him, from what he reckoned was a safe distance. When Peter didn't stir he shouted again, even more loudly. But there was no response. He knew then he was either unconscious or dead, and that he couldn't wait for help to arrive.

To be a paramedic is to be the bottom line. You are the one they all turn to in an emergency and it is no use looking around for somebody else. In the end, it is all down to you.

He decided he had to go in and get the casualty out quickly. He was only going in once, so he was going to bring him out, no matter what.

He went back to the ambulance and put on all the clothes he could, including the big reflective jacket and his gloves. He wrapped a towel out of the back round his head. He pulled out the trolley and rolled it up the side of the house. For a moment he stopped there, working up his courage. Then he took one deep breath and ran across the lawn.

As soon as he crouched down beside Peter the bees were on him. He had told himself he had to stay cool; if he didn't irritate them they wouldn't sting him. After all, they weren't supposed to be aggressive creatures.

Staying cool wasn't easy when he could see at close quarters how Peter had been stung, and feel them landing on his own head. He could feel the vibrations through his scalp and the surging noise of their beating wings was in his ears. He tried to control his panic.

He ducked his own head close to Peter's and called to him again. This time Peter reacted. Not much more than a groan, but it showed that he was at least alive. He wasn't sure how to handle him because the bees were still piled up on the upper half of his body, just like a human beehive. He pulled the trolley closer and wondered how he was going to lift him without the same thing happening to him.

At that moment Dave arrived with the old beekeeper from next door. It had taken him some time to attract his attention because he had been so deeply engrossed in checking over his hives. The old man had brought round his smoke gun and immediately used it to try to clear the bees off Peter's body.

It was only partially successful, and many of the bees just moved on to the other men. Yet somehow, in that cloud of bees, the three of them managed to load Peter on to the trolley and roll him round to the side of the house.

The priority was to get Peter to hospital in the fastest possible time. But they had to spend valuable minutes clearing the rest of the bees off him, and off themselves. They didn't want to risk any of them getting into the ambulance; it is drummed into all

'To be a paramedic is to be the bottom line. You are the one they all turn to in an emergency and it is no use looking around for somebody else. In the end, it is all down to you'

'Peter was moving in and out of consciousness and moaning'

ambulancemen that the vehicle has to be kept as a safe environment for the casualty.

It wasn't easy, but eventually they got them all off. They almost threw the trolley into the back of the ambulance, and closed the doors on a nightmare.

As they set off, Peter started vomiting violently, a reaction to the shock and the large amount of poison in his bloodstream from the stings. He was moving in and out of consciousness and moaning. Dave moved him on to his side to stop him choking. He put him on oxygen, and inserted a needle into one of his veins so the doctors at the hospital could administer drugs as soon as they got there.

It was up to them now. Dave crossed his fingers.

The hospital had been warned what to expect. But they did not know whether Peter's condition was due to a special allergic reaction, or the extent of toxin in his blood.

As soon as he arrived they gave him extra oxygen to help him with his breathing. Then they fed three different types of drugs into the tube that was already inserted in his vein. The first was adrenalin, which occurs naturally in the body and counteracts the allergic reaction to stings and other forms of shock. Next, they gave him an antihistamine drug to work against the venom in the stings, which contains a form of histamine. And lastly they dosed him with a steroid drug which is useful in dampening down allergic reaction, but takes an hour or two to start to work.

They still didn't know how critical his condition was because anaphylactic shock need not happen suddenly. Sometimes it takes hours to reach its full effect. When it does happen, it is acute and dangerous. Breathing is choked off by swelling in the upper airway and an asthma-like reaction in the lungs. It affects all the rest of the body, too; all the blood vessels dilate and the blood pressure drops as a result.

It can easily be fatal, but it is so rare that nobody in the accident and emergency department could remember seeing a case. They watched, and they waited.

Peter came to and vomited again, before lapsing back into unconsciousness. But the sharp deterioration they had feared did not happen. His condition stabilized and he moved out of danger as his body absorbed the poison from so many stings.

He did not wake up until he was on the ward. The first thing he saw was a nurse sitting next to him picking stings out of his hair. She had already taken more than a hundred from his head and neck, and laid them out on a white sheet. He only thought was: 'My God, I'm alive.'

For two or three days he felt awful because so much bee venom was still in his system. For more than a fortnight he had a tightness in his chest and severe cramps that were treated with quinine tablets.

Before he went back to work there was one thing he felt he had to do. He walked down to a flowering bush at the end of his garden which was covered in bees, and pushed his hand among the flowerheads. He forced himself to hold his hand steady and let two or three bees walk across it. It was, he says, like getting back on a motorbike after a crash. He couldn't allow what had happened to him to develop into a phobia.

Later he took it a step further and went round to the garden next door to stand next to the hives. He stood just aside from the flight path of the bees as they came and went. It took a lot of courage, but it worked. He has conquered his fear; there are no lasting ill-effects, physical or psychological.

He doesn't blame the bees, or the beekeeper. His main feeling after coming so close to dying in his own back garden on that fine summer evening is gratitude. An overwhelming need to thank the ambulance crew who risked themselves to rescue him.

The bottom line that saved his life.

Bee experts still don't know why Peter was attacked. Normally bees will sting only when they feel their colony is under attack, and it is rare to suffer multiple stings at any distance from the hive.

Sometimes a change in the weather, a sudden deterioration after a sunny day that reduces the honey flow, will make them irritable. Maybe it was something about the way Peter smelt, the scent of a shampoo or soap, for instance, that annoyed them. The bees did not appear to be swarming. When they swarm, and a new queen sets out with her followers to found a separate colony, they are normally good-natured and easy for the beekeeper to handle. The expert we consulted had never heard of an incident like this in thirty years.

Bee Stings

If you are attacked by a bee or a swarm of bees, don't wave your hands and arms around. Bees have a compound eye that multiplies sharp movements. You will only antagonize them.

A bee sting is barbed and the bee usually cannot remove it. It gets left behind, complete with the poison sac and muscles and nerves that are still pumping venom into you. So don't pick it off with tweezers; rather, scrape it away with a knife as soon as you can and that will reduce the amount of venom you receive.

You should cool the area where you have been stung, preferably with ice. That will take away the pain, reduce the swelling, and constrict the blood vessels, which will slow the rate at which the venom is absorbed into the body. You can slow it still further if you raise the part of the body where you have been stung – by putting your arm in a sling, for instance.

If you are stung by more than ten bees at the same time, there may be other effects from the higher dosage of toxin. If you've suffered badly from a bee sting in the past, or you're prone to allergies, see your doctor, who can give you a syringe of adrenalin you can carry round at all times.

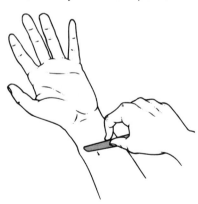

If you're stung by a bee quickly scrape it away with your fingernail or a knife.

What to do if you are attacked by a swarm of bees

● **Move slowly** indoors or into undergrowth. Bees prefer sunlight to shade.

● **Crouch down** and cover your head with your arms to stop your face being badly stung. Bees tend to aim for the highest point and will become confused.

● **Don't kill any bees.** When they're squashed they release a hormone to signal danger. The presence of this pheromone increases the chances that the swarm will attack.

● In rare cases the venom pumped into you when you're stung triggers an extreme allergic reaction called anaphylactic shock. This reaction causes substances to be released into the blood that dilate the vessels and constrict air passages. This makes breathing difficult and blood pressure falls dramatically.

If this happens call for help immediately – you'll need an injection of **adrenalin** as soon as possible.

CHAPTER 9

The Luckiest Man Alive

They heard the explosion five miles away. It sounded like a huge bomb going off, but it wasn't; it was Alec Anderson, using up the eighth of his nine lives.

There is a scientific explanation for how he survived that day, but most of his friends just believe it was a miracle. And it was those friends who were there, watched it all happen, and got him out alive.

999 RECONSTRUCTION 'The entire wheelhouse had been thrown fifteen feet into the air, and it was still in one piece when it came down right on top of him'

Anstruther is a pretty place, one of a string of picturesque fishing villages that turn their back on the depressed region of Fife, and face south-east into the North Sea where generation after generation of their sons have earned their living. It is a poor one, in these days of overfishing and quotas. Fewer than half a dozen boats still operate out of Anstruther, working the lobsters and the prawns. Still, it looks and feels like a fishing community: close-knit, hard working and resourceful, where people can rely on each other in a crisis.

Alec Anderson was a fisherman, and everybody knew him in Anstruther. He had a reputation for luck, for getting out of what he called 'scrapes'. He had been knocked down by a bus, and by a car, and survived. Twice he had gone overboard from a trawler which most fishermen regard as an automatic death sentence. That day in October, though, he excelled himself.

For a long time he had acted as mate on his brother-in-law's boat but, a couple of years before, he had raised the money to buy his own. The *Stand Sure* was a forty-foot prawn trawler, an old vessel, cranky and temperamental. But with so many fishermen going after the prawns these days, and the prices so low, there was not enough money in it to justify a new boat. Keeping it going was a full-time job in itself. When the leaks in the hull got too bad, he resigned himself to a few days in port for running repairs.

The previous Saturday he had shifted the *Stand Sure* across from her normal berth, on the middle pier next to the lifeboat shed, to lie behind the harbourmaster's office. It was as good as a dry dock there when the tide went out. Beached, but wedged upright against the side of the pier.

He had turned that short trip across the harbour into a party for the kids. The boat was full of them, three of his own, his cousin's two, his sister's child and all their pals. The accident could easily have happened then.

They all go cold now, just thinking about it.

It was the Tuesday afterwards, mid-morning, and Alec had already been working on the boat for a couple of hours. His wife, Heather, was coming down to the shops anyway, and looked in for a cup of tea. Alec had run out of milk and Heather said she would go over to the Co-op to buy some, if he would put the kettle on.

> 'Alec Anderson was a fisherman, and everybody knew him in Anstruther. He had a reputation for luck, for getting out of what he called "scrapes" … That day in October, though, he excelled himself'

She had just crossed to the cash desk to pay for it, when there was an almighty explosion outside. The door to the Co-op slammed open, and something seemed to suck all the air out of the shop. Outside, a great cloud of debris just hung over the harbour, as if everything was happening in slow motion. Heather dropped her basket and ran for the door. Then the screaming began.

It is a strange thing that the man at the centre of that enormous blast, which was heard up and down the Fife coast and several miles inland, did not hear it at all.

Alec had gone down into the little galley and filled up the kettle. He took out his lighter and, when he flicked it, ignited a fireball.

The cabin was instantly filled with flame, and then the whole boat seemed to cave in around him. A rushing noise took all the flames away, and Alec's world disintegrated around him. He had a moment's thought that he would be burned to death, before the wreckage came back down and buried him.

He lay in the bilges, under the ruins of the *Stand Sure*, and told himself this was it. He used the Fifers' slang word for something that is finished, clapped out, dead. 'Talibanja,' he said to himself. 'Talibanja. The luck's run out.'

The pipes that led from the LPG cylinder to the stove in the galley had always been corroded, and must have been leaking for some time. The gas is heavier than air and had settled in the bilges. Slowly, insidiously, it had filled up the lower half of the boat, waiting for the tiniest of sparks to blow it to smithereens.

The enormous force of the explosion blasted the hull flat, and opened it along its seams just like a kipper. It blew the deck to pieces and flung it high into the air. What came down was a mass of little more than firewood; afterwards they could barely find any piece more than a yard long.

Alec had somehow escaped being killed by the force of the initial explosion, and was now entombed by the falling wreckage, on his stomach, in what was left of the bottom of the boat. That should have finished him, but for another extraordinary stroke of luck.

The entire wheelhouse had been thrown fifteen feet into the air, and it was still in one piece when it came down right on top of him. It made a bridge across the top of his body without giving him a fatal blow, and then protected his body from the rest of the wreckage. He was in no position to realize it then, but his luck had been working overtime.

It was working for the whole place. That time of the morning Anstruther harbour is often packed, with tourists as well as locals. The explosion shattered shop windows 200 yards away and swept the harbour front with sharp pieces of wood and metal. It might have killed and injured scores of people. But for some reason, or maybe no reason at all, there was hardly anybody about when Alec stooped over his stove with his lighter. He was the only real casualty.

Across the harbour, the crew of the Anstruther lifeboat were gathered together on its deck mostly looking the other way when the explosion happened. They all whirled round in time to see the bits of the *Stand Sure* still hanging in the air. Peter Murray, the coxswain, watched the debris rise and then fall back to rain down on what was left of the boat's hull with a great, rattling noise, almost as loud as the explosion itself.

It was yet another of the odd coincidences that day that the whole lifeboat crew should have been assembled before the emergency even happened. They were doing trials on their new, Mersey Class lifeboat, the *Kingdom of Fife*. In a town like Anstruther the lifeboat is an institution. Everybody had helped to raise the £600,000 it had cost. And everybody had turned out back in August to welcome it into harbour for the first time. Hundreds lined the quay, the pipers were out, and the drink flowed after the minister gave the boat a blessing. Now they were practising launching and recovering it in the harbour, under the eyes of the inspectors of the Royal National Lifeboat Institution. They had just recovered it for the second time on to its carriage, worked it up to the top of the slip by the shed, when a real emergency got in the way.

Peter Murray and his men had dropped everything and were heading for the scene of the accident on the opposite side of the harbour before the noise of the explosion had died away. They had to push their way through a growing crowd of people. Among them was Alec's wife, Heather, who was rooted to the spot on the pier looking down on what had been her husband's boat, terrified at what might have happened to him. He should have been on deck, she thought. But there wasn't a deck any more. Just a wheelhouse, still recognizable in a mangle of wood and iron.

Coxswain Peter Murray had seen some grim sights, but nothing like this. He could not believe how anyone could have survived that kind of explosion, and surely nobody would ever get out of a pile of wreckage like that. Yet, as he got nearer, he saw a man standing on the pier directly above the boat, pointing down and saying, over and over, 'There's somebody in there.'

Peter jumped on to what was left of the boat and pushed forward through the debris, the rest of the crew at his heels. It was so badly damaged he did not even know which boat it was. One of his men had to tell him it was the *Stand Sure*, Alec Anderson's boat. They all knew it, and him, but now the wheelhouse was the only thing they could recognize.

Sticking out from underneath the wheelhouse, the coxswain found a hand. And the hand was moving.

He had to clear away piles of rubble to be able to bend down and shout through the broken decking, 'Can your hear me?'

'Aye, I can hear you.' Peter recognized Alec's rich, east coast brogue instantly.

He picked up Alec's hand. It was blistered and burnt. He asked him if he could feel him touching his hand, and he said he could feel his hands, but not his legs and feet. He sounded panicky, but rational. Peter was still finding it difficult to believe anybody could have survived at all. A miracle, he thought, no other word for it.

He looked over his shoulder and saw his crew rushing around the wheelhouse, trying to shore it up with any bits of wood and metal they could lay their hands on.

It might take another miracle to get him out.

Alec Anderson's first memory after the explosion was fear; a terrible fear that he would be burned to death. The flames still seemed to sear his eyes, and the conscious part of his mind was telling him how unlucky he was that the boat was high and dry, with no water to put the fire out. He was not rational enough to realize that if the boat *had* been in the water, he would have already drowned.

He had heard his wife screaming. He had felt the lifeboat crew jump on board, and could hear Peter Murray now, shouting up to Heather to say he was all right. He did not feel all right, and if the

'He picked up Alec's hand. It was blistered and burnt. He said he could feel his hands, but not his legs and feet'

boat caught fire again he was dead. He wondered how long it would take them to get him free.

He ought to have trusted his luck. It was still working hard for him. Tuesday was the local doctor's day off, so Dr Chris Brittain was in town, not out visiting miles away somewhere in the broad hinterland of his practice. And he was not just an ordinary GP either. Dr Brittain was a 'BASICS' doctor, a member of the British Association of Immediate Care. He was specially trained to deal with emergencies, with a wide experience of accident and trauma medicine; he had even been a regular member of the lifeboat crew. It would be hard to imagine anybody better qualified to help Alec, and he was just round the corner when the boat blew up.

It was looking like a quiet day, and Dr Brittain was just getting some cash from the machine outside the bank when he heard the explosion. He knew at once it was far too big to be a car or a boat backfiring, and jumped in his car to head for the harbour.

When he got there it was in chaos. There was wreckage and broken glass all over the road and the pier. It was so bad he had to abandon the car and run to get to where the explosion had happened. The lifeboat crew had only just climbed on board when he reached the edge of the pier and looked down.

The first thing he saw was the hand, and for a few, horrifying seconds thought it had been detached from the rest of the body, blown off by the blast. But then he could see the lifeboat coxswain talking to somebody, and he realized the hand was moving.

Alec was far back under the wheelhouse; Peter Murray and Dr Brittain began working inwards towards him through piles of wood that were sodden with diesel and water. They gradually eased out a piece at a time to uncover more of his body. The decking was very unstable. Each time they tried to remove a big section it would move and hurt him.

Slowly they worked their way up his arm. They managed to get to his neck and uncover most of his head. Dr Britain could see that he was quite badly burnt, but was more concerned then about other injuries. He pushed himself further into the hole he had made, and tried to ignore the nails that poked into him from all angles.

He kept being surprised at how few injuries Alec seemed to have.

As he felt his way along the parts of his body he could reach he expected to find broken bones, internal injuries. As far as he could check, half hanging, half lying in the claustrophobic gloom under the wreckage, there was none. But Alec still said he could not feel his legs, and that was a bad sign. It could mean his back was broken and he was paralysed. Every time the wreckage moved it could be doing him permanent damage. It was important to get him out quickly, but one mistake might kill him.

Alec was in pain but Dr Brittain was afraid to give him morphine because he needed Alec to stay alert. Dr Brittain was also concerned that he might have a head injury. He managed to push a face mask down to him so that he could breathe in a milder, painkilling gas called Entonox. It was not having much effect. Alec's face was burnt, which made it difficult for him to get a seal round his mouth and nose.

This is what hell must be like, he thought. Everything was black, except for a few cracks in the piles of wreckage around him. He could just see the pier through what used to be the port side of his boat, and there was a thin strip of daylight on the starboard side. The light from the hatch above him was mostly blotted out by the bulk of the doctor leaning down over him. All around, what was left of his boat creaked and groaned as the splintered beams and broken metal shifted under the weight of those working to free him. Why couldn't they hurry up? How long was he going to have to lie there?

And why couldn't the doctor shut up for a moment? Talk, talk, talk, trying to cheer him up. He didn't want to be cheered up, he wanted to get out.

There was a point to all the talking; Dr Brittain was trying to keep him conscious, and keeping a running check on his condition by seeing how alert he was.

But Alec was frightened and irritable. As far as he was concerned it was just prattling, and it was not helping to get him free. He was even talking about the weather, for God's sake. He couldn't bother his backside about the weather! All he could think was: 'Shut up, and get me out.'

It was not as simple as that. The wheelhouse and the rest of the wreckage on top of him was still very unstable, and it would be a complex operation to lift it. The lifeboat crew and Anstruther's part-time firemen, who had arrived shortly afterwards, did their

'This is what hell must be like, he thought. Everything was black, except for a few cracks in the piles of wreckage around him'

best to shore it all up, but they realized they would need more equipment, more expertise.

It was a senior, full-time fireman, from Methil down the coast, who took charge. Assistant Divisional Officer Dougie Welsh was an old-style firefighter, a practical man with years of experience. At first glance from the dockside, all that experience told him that this operation was not going to be a rescue, but a depressing search for a body. For once, he was wrong.

They shouted up from the boat that the owner was still alive, and when he got down there he found Dr Brittain alongside the casualty, talking to him. The situation, which had looked so bad from the dockside, began to seem more manageable. There was a good team of men already working trying to stabilize the wreckage; he had a trauma expert, whom he knew and trusted, looking after the patient; and the patient himself was not so badly injured that he would have to be removed straightaway, whatever the risk.

The doctor still had reservations about Alec's back, but, as far as he could see, his injuries were not life-threatening. And, even though he was pinned down, there did not seem to be severe crush injuries either. They would have been a real worry because toxins would have built up in his compressed tissues ready to be released into the bloodstream when the weight was lifted off, throwing him into deep – and possibly fatal – shock. Somehow, the wreckage had collapsed back all over Alec without doing him serious damage. It all gave Dougie Welsh a little more time to plan the operation. And he needed it, because it would not be easy.

For a moment, he considered trying to cut through the timber work of the hull to reach Alec from underneath. But he quickly realized it would be too dangerous. With the boat in such a mess it was difficult to pinpoint exactly where the casualty was from outside, and there was a risk they would injure him with the cutting equipment. Also they would be cutting into an already unstable structure; it might all collapse round their ears.

The only sensible option was to try to lift the whole wheelhouse in one section. It would have to be done very slowly to try to keep it intact; if it came to pieces it could kill anybody underneath. They could not use jacks, because there was nothing solid to rest them on. They needed a crane, and a lot of luck.

The crane was already on its way; and Alec's luck was still in.

His temper wasn't. He was a hard-headed, practical and obstinate man and it did not look to him as if they were getting on with it as fast as they should be. He knew nearly all of them; two of the firemen were his cousins, he knew all the lifeboatmen, the doctor had treated him and his family for years. They kept reassuring him, but he wasn't having any of it. He heard them talking among themselves and felt they were ignoring him. He was cursing and swearing, giving them all mouthfuls of abuse.

The firemen were used to it; not many people act like angels when they're trapped by an accident that should have killed them. And nobody ever called any Fife fisherman an angel.

Anyway, there was not much they could do until the crane arrived.

It was already on the outskirts of Anstruther, an unwieldy vehicle slightly larger than a bus, trying to squeeze through the narrow roads and parked cars to get to the harbour. Russell Robertson was driving it. He did not know what to expect, nor that it would be his skill which would decide whether a man would live or die.

He had been lifting an engine into a boat at the little yard at St Monance five miles along the coast, when the call came through from the Anstruther harbourmaster. He did not stop to ask many questions. He uncoupled the lift, pulled the crane jib in, retracted the legs, gathered up as much equipment as he thought he would need, and set off at the stately forty miles an hour that was all the old crane could manage.

They had cleared a space for him near what was left of the *Stand Sure*. By the time he arrived the lifeboat crew had used the bits of rope left in the wreckage to start rigging up a bridle around the wheelhouse so that it could be lifted. The ropes had been in big coils in the stern of the boat by the nets before the explosion, but had now been blown all over the place. The lifeboatmen cut them up and wrapped them around the deck beams that were still attached to the wheelhouse and gave the best chance of lifting the whole thing in one go.

Dougie Welsh felt a great weight of responsibility settle on his shoulders as the time came for them to start the lift. He was thinking to himself that this was a worst-case scenario. Normally when they were rescuing somebody they could seldom make the situation worse. But here they had a casualty who, by some miracle, had survived a major incident with only minimal injuries. Their rescue operation had only to go slightly wrong and he would be badly injured, or even killed.

Still, he thought, responsibility is what I am paid for.

He ordered everybody but his firemen off the boat, even Dr Brittain. He could not justify the risk to those he called 'civilians'. He posted one of his experienced firemen, Station Officer Ian Kelly, alongside Alec so he would know his condition and what was happening to him. He explained his instructions carefully, and put himself where he could see both the wheelhouse and the pier.

When they were ready to go he called for quiet. Hundreds of people had gathered in the harbour and he could not run the risk of missing a shouted warning that things were going wrong.

The only way it could succeed was to bring up the wheelhouse an inch or two at a time. Lift it a fraction, then push in supports to stop it collapsing back again, or falling apart. Then lift it again, and keep on doing it in tiny movements until Alec was free.

For Russell Robertson it was the ultimate test of skill. He could not see, directly, what was happening; he was working at the end of a long chain of command. He could see a fireman on the pier who was relaying signals from Dougie Welsh. He, in turn, was looking to Ian Kelly down in the hull next to the casualty. Fire service custom was to keep quiet unless you had something important to say, but Dougie had told Ian to keep talking. He wanted to know everything that was happening; he even took hold of Ian's leg so that he could feel from his reactions if things were going wrong even before he opened his mouth.

All Russell Robertson had to work with was a small lever, and the instinct developed over the years for the precise moment when it would engage and start to lift the load.

The first lift worked perfectly. The wheelhouse came up two or three inches and the firemen rushed in to pack it with wedges and air bags. Alec was able to move the arm that had been trapped until then and change position under the wreckage. At last he could straighten his legs, and the feeling came flooding back to them.

It was the second lift when it started to go wrong.

The wheelhouse was already on a slight angle and, as they started to lift it for the second time, it moved suddenly sideways. Alec thought the whole thing was coming down on top of him and

started screaming. Dougie called an immediate halt even though it was difficult to tell from the outside what had happened.

It had been frightening for those down below and gave everybody involved in the operation a scare by underlining how fragile the situation was. They stabilized the wheelhouse as best they could, and prepared for the third lift.

The space around Alec was getting bigger and the fright he had just had made him even more desperate to get out. The doctor, down on the beach below him, kept telling him to lie still, but as soon as he thought he could move there was no stopping him. He twisted up, practically threw Ian Kelly out of the way, and, as far as the crowd was concerned, popped up out of the hull like a rabbit out of a hole.

It was a combination of shock, fear and maybe the gas he had been given. Whatever the reason, the man everybody had expected to be near death, or at least paralysed, actually ran down the wreckage of his boat and was about to throw himself off the end onto the beach until the firemen managed to restrain him. They helped him down, and the doctor took his arm to try to support

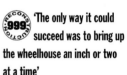 'The only way it could succeed was to bring up the wheelhouse an inch or two at a time'

him up the beach. But he shook them all off and went to his wife.

Bliss, pure bliss, he thought, to be standing up in the open air, out of it all. The way the crowd was cheering you would think he was Jesus, risen from the dead. He looked back at his boat and could not believe he had walked away from all that hellish mess. He was desperate for a cigarette, but let himself be laid down on a stretcher and buckled in to the ambulance for the short journey to hospital.

There, the burns on his hand and face were found to be only superficial. They hurt like the devil but that, they told him, was a good sign. He had a few bruises, including a big one round his kidneys, but he was otherwise unscathed. They let him go the following morning.

For two or three months afterwards he could not sleep very well, going over and over in his mind what might have happened if the tide had been in, if the flames had not been blown out by the explosion, if it had happened when all the kids were on board. The doctor said he should have some therapy, but he didn't and eventually he managed to put it behind him.

The fire service investigated the explosion and pieced together the factors that enabled Alec to survive, so unique a pattern of events as to amount to a statistical miracle.

When he lit the gas that had built up, he was at the exact centre of the explosion, so all the debris was moving away from him. If he had been hit by even a splinter at the speeds produced by the blast he would have been killed there and then.

The fact that the hull ruptured and opened up along its seams allowed the blast wave to escape, so Alec did not suffer the normal blast injuries, the ear and lung damage that so often prove fatal.

And then he was so extraordinarily fortunate with the position he was in among the wreckage. The explosion threw the upper section of the hull straight up in the air and the most crucial part of it came down in one piece over Alec, who had fallen into a void under the wreckage of the deck.

Anstruther is a small place and Alec sees his rescuers every day. He has had plenty of opportunities to thank them, and apologize for his language that day. There is only one thing that irritates him.

He does so wish that people would stop telling him how lucky he is.

(Opposite) Once free Alec 'actually ran down the wreckage of his boat and was about to throw himself off the end onto the beach until the firemen managed to restrain him'

CHAPTER 10

The Gentle Giant

They don't often build statues to animals. But, in years to come, the visitors to Jersey Zoo in the Channel Islands will find a life-size bronze of a huge ape given pride of place near the large gorilla enclosure.

'He looked up, curiously, at the crowd and leaned over Levan, as if to protect him'

The statue will commemorate one particular animal, arguably the world's most famous gorilla. He was the first male to be born in captivity; the first to be raised by his mother rather than hand-reared by keepers; and he fathered more offspring himself than any other gorilla ever recorded. More than two dozen of his grandchildren, in that enclosure as well as many others across the world, help preserve his species as it becomes increasingly rare in its native habitat, the jungle ranges of western Africa.

But none of this is why he became so celebrated, nor why people came from all over the world to see him in particular. He became famous one day in August when a little boy fell into his enclosure. A boy who fell into the power of an animal stronger than ten men, which could tear a horse limb from limb, and which, to many, was the very embodiment of ferocity as well as strength.

Yet when he had a helpless child at his feet, he seemed as caring and protective as a human father. It was all captured on an amateur's video camera, and changed the way people in many different countries felt about the big apes.

Not that Jambo was the real hero that day. Brian Fox, the ambulanceman who had to conquer his terror and bring the boy out, was the brave one.

But it's the gorilla they remember. It's the gorilla they will be raising the statue to, with the plaque underneath, and the name by which he will always be known: 'Jambo, the Gentle Giant'.

The Merritt family had been to Jersey Zoo in the past, but that was before Lloyd, the youngest, was born. They had all talked about it a lot, so it was natural he would want to go too when they went to the Channel Islands on their family summer holiday. It was Lloyd's birthday that day and they were a bit bored with the beach. He deserved a treat, everybody else was keen, so off they went.

Jersey Zoo was founded by the naturalist, Gerald Durrell, as more than just a place to go and gawp at captured animals. It's a protected home for endangered species. Steve and Pauline Merritt explained to the four children that the animals they were seeing might well have died out in the wild by the time they grew up. They were all very young and excited so it was difficult to know how much they were taking in, but it was an ideal outing anyway.

Stephanie, Clint, Levan and Lloyd (they were all named after Hollywood stars, Levan after Lee Van Cleef) liked the rare birds;

they liked the golden lion tamarind monkeys from Brazil even more, particularly when one tried to urinate on their dad's shirt. They were sweet little creatures, with appealing marmoset faces. But the kids really wanted to see something dangerous.

Then Stephanie spotted the gorillas.

From where they were, near the top of the hill, they could look down on the gorilla compound and see what Stephanie called 'the really big monkeys' ambling around it. As they got closer, though, they lost sight of them behind the surrounding wall.

The techniques for keeping big animals have come a long way since the first gorillas were held in captivity, a century or more ago. They used to be kept penned up in tiny barred cages. Now things are done differently, particularly at Jersey. There, the gorilla compound is a large open area, with small hillocks and other natural features. The animals are kept from the spectators, and vice versa, by a deep ditch surmounted by a low wall. The animals are happier; the spectators feel safe, even though there are no bars between them and some of the strongest animals on earth.

When the Merritt family got to the compound the gorillas had moved to their side of the enclosure, under the wall. The only way to see them properly was to lean right over. The younger children couldn't get a glimpse of them at all.

Steve Merritt lifted Lloyd up to give him a better view. There's some confusion about what happened then. Steve himself thinks he helped Levan on to the wall and was distracted for a moment. However it happened, Pauline turned to see Levan, bolt upright on top of the wall just as he toppled forward. Steve was looking at her and, in that fraction of a second, could see what was happening by the expression on her face.

The next few moments were a blur of screaming and shouting Steve tried to climb over the wall, but was stopped by the people around him. Pauline lost control completely, and had hysterics. She did not get to see where he had fallen. Two or three people kept her away from the edge and took her to the café, trying to reassure her that he had fallen on to grass, and that the gorillas were all locked away in their secure quarters at the other end of the compound. They were wrong on both counts.

Steve was being held back by some of the spectators, but he could see what had happened to his five-year-old son. He had fallen just over twelve feet on to a pathway that runs round the inner edge of the compound. He was lying perfectly still, with blood coming from the back of his head. They didn't know, at that stage, that Levan had struck his head against the wall as he had fallen, and fractured his skull. Steve stopped struggling to free himself because he really thought the boy was dead. Levan didn't move, even when the first of the gorillas walked up to him.

The crowd watched in horror as the whole troop of gorillas, animals they had been conditioned to regard as little short of monsters, moved in on the boy. Gorillas can be aggressive when they are threatened, and the reaction of the crowd was making the situation dangerously charged. The first animal to approach the child was nervous and there was a chance it might injure him, even without intending any harm.

That's when Jambo took charge.

Jambo was the dominant male of the group, the adult 'silverback', with the grey ruff of maturity in his stiff fur. He weighed nearly thirty stone. He was solid muscle and possibly no animal on earth could have lasted more than a few minutes with him if he had lost his temper. Yet the impression he gave, as he shooed his concubines away from the boy's body, was of power under control. The great ape was gentle.

Jambo settled on his haunches beside Levan and stroked his back, in what could only be interpreted as worried concern. He pulled his shirt down, like a parent would. He touched him with one of those great black hands and sniffed the ends of his fingers trying to work out what it was that had intruded into his territory. He looked up, curiously, at the crowd and leaned over Levan, as if to protect him.

There were many in the crowd who felt it was only a matter of time before the gorillas killed the child. There was a lot of screaming when Jambo got close to him. Several people said they should throw rocks at the animals. Others said the keepers should shoot them, or put them to sleep with anaesthetic darts.

As luck would have it, the gorilla keeper was off-duty at the time of the incident. But it was obvious to the relief keeper, Andy Wood, and the other zoo officials who had gathered at the enclosure, that nothing the crowd was yelling for would do any good. Throwing stones at the gorillas would only make them aggressive and increase the risk to the boy. Shooting them could only be a last resort and,

'Jambo settled on his haunches beside Levan and stroked his back, in what could only be interpreted as worried concern' because there were so many of the animals, could not be done quickly enough to ensure Levan's safety in any case. The same applied to tranquillizing the animals. That was an even longer procedure. It would take time to set up the blowpipes and the darts; the animals could react badly, and the drugs would take anything up to a quarter of an hour to put each gorilla to sleep.

The irony was that the greatest threat to Levan at that moment was the crowd. Jambo had the situation in the pit under his own massive control, keeping the other gorillas away and the whole troop quiet. But the spectators could have changed all that in an instant, if somebody did something stupid. Steve Merritt had tried to get into the pit himself, and several other people had talked of it. Jambo obviously did not regard an unconscious child as any sort of threat. But adult humans showing aggression towards him on his own territory could well have provoked a very different response.

'There was a lot of screaming when Jambo got close to him'

The zookeepers' first step was to keep the humans calm. Then they worked on a plan to lure the animals away.

All this time people had been shouting Levan's name. A nurse in the crowd had come up to Steve and told him they had to try to wake him, to stop him slipping into the coma of deep shock. He had started calling to him and others had joined in. For more than ten minutes the shouting had no effect. Then, as if he was waking from a long sleep, Levan rolled slightly sideways, opened his eyes, and screamed.

Levan cannot remember seeing the gorillas down in the pit. He might not have been fully conscious. It could well be that the blow on his head had blurred his vision so much that he could make nothing of his surroundings. Or, perhaps, the shock of waking up and seeing an enormous gorilla leaning over him was too much for his brain to accept, and it has been wiped from his memory.

The gorillas were shocked, too. The boy's crying upset them all. The troop shied away, and even Jambo retreated a few steps, looking puzzled and wary.

Up until then the keepers' efforts to lure the animals away had not worked. They had put food out to persuade them to go back to their shelter but it had been ignored. Now, though, Jambo led them away from Levan; he even went back to round up a female gorilla which had stayed behind for a closer look at the boy. The keepers managed to usher them inside, thinking they had solved the problem.

But as they did so, a young male gorilla, which had been kept back inside while the others had been allowed out, dashed through the doors and out into the enclosure.

In some ways, the situation was worse now. There was only one gorilla at large but, instead of the mature and good-natured Jambo, and his troop of obedient females, they now had to deal with the ape equivalent of a wild teenager.

Hobbit, at that time, was eight, still black in the back without any trace of silver fur. But he already weighed over seventeen stone and was capable of doing enormous damage. He was kept away from Jambo; they were not allowed to run together in the enclosure because they would fight for dominance of the group.

He was excitable and raced backwards and forwards across the enclosure. There was no way a bunch of bananas was going to lure him back into the cages.

Pauline Merritt couldn't remember how many cups of tea she had had, but she wasn't going to be kept in the cafeteria any longer. They had come and told her the gorillas were all safely inside, and that Levan was conscious now. She insisted on seeing for herself.

At first they kept her back on the grass bank where she couldn't see very much. But she was in such a state they eventually let her look over the wall.

What she saw made her panic worse. Levan had again stopped moving. There was blood all around his head and trickling across the concrete pathway. Pauline could see no sign of him breathing and was convinced he was dead.

His arm was broken; the bones were sticking out and his hand was wrenched round, as if it was about to fall off. Pauline kept shouting, hysterically, over and over again, 'Look at his hand. Look at his hand.' Just as they were trying to pull her back from the wall again, Levan stirred and tried to get up and she shouted to him to stay down. Then she was taken away.

At the time she was looking down into the pit, Hobbit was racing around on the other side of the enclosure, and she did not see him. She remembers thinking, 'Thank God there are no gorillas loose.' Those around her managed to keep up the pretence that no animal had ever come near him. In order to distract her, two policemen even took her round to the cages to show her the gorillas feeding behind the plate glass. She believed them, and didn't find out the truth until the following day.

She could not understand why nobody was getting Levan out. The truth was that it took a brave man to face a gorilla to rescue the boy.

He was just driving in through the front gates.

They had joked as they climbed into the ambulance and drove through the twisting island roads towards the zoo. It was Brian Fox's turn to be the attendant, and he was the one who collected the message from the control room window. René Connon was driver that day, and was already warming up the vehicle.

Most emergency calls don't turn out to be that serious, and a child falling into the gorilla pit sounded like a joke. Even if it wasn't, they were bound to have got the gorillas out by the time they arrived and they would just have a straightforward minor injury to deal with. René concentrated on winding Brian up. If he jumped in the gorilla pit, he told them, all the gorillas would jump out. Either that, or they would recognize him as one of their own and invite him for tea. All light-hearted stuff – but they did not know then what they were heading for.

Two keepers were making their way into the enclosure by the time the ambulance arrived. The relief keeper, Andy Wood, went first, armed with a borrowed policeman's truncheon. He had only stood in for the main gorilla keeper on odd days. He hadn't had the chance to form a relationship with the gorillas and hadn't had to go in with one like this before.

The second keeper had even less experience with gorillas. He was the bird expert. He did not know what he would do with the bit of broom handle he had picked up, but he went in all the same.

Hobbit raced backwards and forwards as the keepers tried to get themselves between him and the boy. He became more agitated, and made as if to attack them. Andy Wood tried to create a positive, confident image and hoped the gorilla would not sense the fear inside. For Hobbit *was* frightening. He was putting on his aggressive display, stamping around, sucking his lips, breaking foliage and looking for all the world as if he was about to pick up both keepers and throw them bodily out of the enclosure. He could have, too.

The experts say most gorilla aggression is bluff, pure theatre. But that's easy to say when you're not staring at an angry one, face to face, with only a bit of stick in your hand.

Brian Fox took it all in from the top of the wall. At that point Levan was on his side, crying. The crowd were upset by the boy's distress, but Brian knew it was a good sign. He was alive, he was conscious, and he was breathing all right. It gave them time to work out a plan.

He got the haversack containing the first-aid kit out of the ambulance, and René collected a rope. They were just working out the options when Levan turned on his back. He wasn't crying any more, and he had stopped moving. A few seconds later and he started to make choking noises. Brian knew then there were no options. Left like that, he could suffocate at any moment. He would have to be turned over and, with the possibility that he might have spinal injuries from the fall, Brian could not let one of the keepers do that.

He would have to face the gorilla himself.

He jumped down into the pit, and his training took over. He pushed the gorilla to the back of his mind and tried to concentrate on the boy. He could see straightaway that his skull was fractured because of the blood coming out of his ears and his nose. The fractured arm was obvious, too; the broken bones were sticking out just above the wrist.

He had to find out if Levan had injured his back before he made any attempt to lift him. If he moved him, and his back was broken, he could cripple him for life.

> 'The experts say most gorilla aggression is bluff . . . but that's easy to say when you're not staring at an angry one, face to face, with only a bit of stick in your hand'

He checked the spine in the proper sequence, starting at Levan's head and working systematically down his back. Only when he was sure his spine was not damaged did he move him on to his side and work on clearing his airway.

When that was done, he had time to take stock of his own situation. Hobbit had been charging up and down all the while he had been treating the boy. They were trapped against the wall while the gorilla rushed in a semi-circle around them. Brian had thought the animal was huge when he was looking down on him from the top of the wall. Close to, he was enormous. Brian could believe the gorilla was as strong as half a dozen men, but he was having trouble believing the other things he had been told to reassure him. Hobbit might be many things, he thought, but no way is he a vegetarian. Brian really thought Hobbit might tear him apart. His face went as white as his shirt, and his hands were trembling.

Every so often the gorilla would lunge past the keepers and run

Brian Fox 'checked the spine in the proper sequence, starting at Levan's head and working systematically down his back'

right up to them. He felt sure he might make a grab for the boy so he hunched himself forward over his body. However strong he is, he thought, he would have more trouble picking up an overweight ambulanceman than a five-year-old boy.

Each time the keepers drove the gorilla away Hobbit would pick up stones to throw at them. He was a remarkably good shot and several times Brian had to duck and cover Levan with his body. The gorilla just wanted them off his territory.

Not half as badly as Brian did.

There was only one possible way out, and that was up the wall. Luckily, Brian's partner, René, was a cliff-rescue instructor and was fixing up a rope to pull them out. Brian was thoroughly scared, but steeled himself to be patient. He had done the course and knew the most important thing was for the rope to be properly set up and secured. The last thing Levan needed was another fall.

At last they dropped the end of the rope down to him. He tied it around himself, and checked that the knot wouldn't slip. Then he picked Levan up and put him carefully on his shoulder. When he was ready he signalled to those on the other end of the rope to start lifting.

One of the keepers chose that moment to give him a helping hand and grabbed hold of his leg. Brian was looking up at the time and thought, 'Oh God, it's the gorilla. It's got me.'

For a second or two he was so scared he thought he would be able to climb the wall without the rope.

He never dared look back. He started shaking once he was in the ambulance with Levan, and couldn't stop. He had seen it in the casualties he had dealt with; he used to explain to them how they would get delayed shock after an accident, and now it was happening to him.

Levan was taken to hospital in Jersey and, because of the seriousness of his head injuries, transferred to a specialist unit in Southampton. The back of his skull was badly damaged. It might well have resulted in death or permanent brain damage if he had been much older but, because he was only five, the bone of his skull was relatively soft.

His mother says he is not quite the happy-go-lucky child he was before he fell into the gorilla pit, but he is able to do most things now. It is just football, and rougher sports where his head might

'For a second or two he was so scared he thought he would be able to climb the wall without the rope'

get hit again, that are ruled out.

It was not until the following morning that Levan's mother realized for the first time that the gorillas had been anywhere near him. She was watching television out of the corner of her eye when the amateur video footage of the incident was shown in a breakfast news programme. The shock was almost worse than the moment when she saw him fall.

The family has got a video and Levan watches it every fortnight or so. The rest of the family don't like watching it, but Levan has something of an obsession about gorillas now. He says he might become a keeper one day.

Brian Fox keeps in touch, at Christmas and Easter and on Levan's birthday. They have met each other several times since it happened. Each in their own way became quite famous, and it is a bond between them.

Not as famous, though, as Jambo. The great gorilla died unexpectedly, in September 1992, of a rupture of the main artery; nobody knows what caused it. He was thirty-one when he died, a shorter lifespan than most gorillas, which normally live into their late thirties or early forties in captivity.

The tributes and enquiries still come into the zoo about him. They are writing a book about him, as well as erecting the statue. In his own way, 'Jambo the Gentle Giant' has become a legend.

Child Safety

Accidents are the biggest single killer of children in the UK after the age of one – on average two children die this way every day. Just a little more thought and a little more care could save them. Children have thousands of accidents serious enough for them to need hospital treatment and more than half of them occur in or around the home, the very place they seek comfort and security. Most of them could have been prevented, especially the more serious accidents – kettle scalds, falls on stairs and from windows, and severe glass injuries.

Young children

Accidents to children aren't the same as accidents to adults. Most of them are to do with their physical and mental development. The kinds of accidents they have depend on their age. When they are very young, they may distinguish between yes and no but they have no concept of danger or risk. They are initially unaware that hot water can scald or that tablets can poison them. As they get older these concepts slowly become clearer and they become capable of understanding safety messages.

By knowing more about child development you can prevent some accidents from happening or take steps to minimize the injuries that can occur.

Putting things in their mouths

All small children put things in their mouths, but it is not until they reach the age of two at the earliest and possibly not until they're three that a child can tell the difference between food and poisonous substances. Children are born with a sense of taste, so very early on they distinguish between pleasant and unpleasant tastes but not harmless and harmful substances.

Falling over

Falls are a natural part of a child's life, a part of learning and exploring the environment, a part of developing their own skills. But they are also the most common type of accident among children and the injuries sustained can vary between a mild bruise and a fracture or severe concussion. The two areas of major concern are falls from buildings, through windows or off balconies, which tend to be severe, and falls on stairs which are very frequent. The

stairs are a particularly dangerous place for very young children, so block them with safety gates, preferably at the top and bottom. And remember that a child should be at least three to walk downstairs without a grown-up.

Road accidents

Road traffic accidents account for more than half of all fatal child accidents in the UK – and more than half of these die as pedestrians. Teach road safety by your own good example. Find a safe place and explain why you have to stop, look and listen, each time you cross the road together. Never let young children cross a road alone. A child should be at least 9 years old and have previous supervised experience before being allowed to cross a quiet street without an adult. Children can't judge the speed or distance of cars and cope with busy traffic until they're 11 or 12.

Children are not little adults, and are naturally imaginative, daring and inquisitive.

Safety Tips

● Make sure children **stop** before they cross roads.

● Ensure windows lock (in case a child falls out) and that you can unlock them (in case of fire).

● Think ahead. As children grow, they acquire new skills from crawling to climbing and running.

● Turn the thermostat on your hot tank down to 54°C so the water isn't hot enough to scald.

● Tidy up clutter and keep floors clear.

Go on a first-aid course so you can deal safely with family cuts and bruises.

The Green Cross Code

1 First find a safe place to cross, then stop.
2 Stand on the pavement near the kerb.
3 Look all round for traffic and listen.
4 If traffic is coming, let it pass. Look all round again.
5 When there is no traffic near, walk straight across the road.
6 Keep looking and listening for traffic while you cross.

CHAPTER 11

The Widowmaker

The search for oil and gas beneath the dark grey waters of the North Sea is one of the most extraordinary stories of the twentieth century. These are not sheltered waters, nor the rolling ocean. The North Sea is nature's cockpit, where the marching weather systems of the Northern Hemisphere swirl and smash together between hostile shores. To produce fuel enough to power whole nations from such a place is an achievement to rank beside putting a man on the moon. Arguably more difficult, certainly more expensive, and demonstrably more dangerous.

'From a helicopter, the way its workers first saw it, the massive structure looked like a child's toy'

Those who commute to work in the small towns perched on top of those great steel and concrete towers are bored more often than they are frightened. Their workplace is often many times the height and weight of St Paul's Cathedral. Computers and satellites have placed it, inch-perfect, on the seabed. It is an impressive symbol of man's intelligence, his wealth, and his triumph over his environment. But he hasn't conquered the North Sea.

Those who work there, who have seen it in its darker moods, have a word for it.

They call it the Widowmaker.

From a helicopter, the way its workers first saw it, the massive structure looked like a child's toy. It was a jack-up rig, which described exactly what it did. It was basically a great barge, with four huge Meccano-style legs at each corner. When it reached the spot where it was to drill for oil or gas, the legs would be cranked down to the seabed to prop it in place. When the operation was over, the legs would be ratcheted up so the rig was floating again, and tugs would tow it to a new location.

That was what was happening one November night, about seventy miles off Great Yarmouth, when the North Sea turned first nasty, then murderous. Within hours, the £30 million drilling rig had gone to the bottom. Its crew would have joined it, but for the heroism and almost superhuman skills of two helicopter crews who flew into a nightmare to rescue them.

The rig manager and his crew had watched the weather forecasts that day with growing concern. The storm was going to catch the rig at the worst possible moment, while it was on the move. It was under tow to a new drilling position within the network of gas fields of the southern North Sea. The rewards of the industry, humming away over the horizon around them, were colossal; it produced gas worth £12 billion a year. But the risks were high, too.

They were about to find that out.

In the beginning, as the storm gathered itself, they had been irritated rather than frightened. A crew change, scheduled for eleven that morning, had been postponed because of the deteriorating weather.

Billy Mitchell, senior electrician on board, knew the crew had been looking forward to an evening drinking ashore in the bars of Great Yarmouth. Now they would have to wait. The forecast talked of storm force eight. God knew when they would get ashore now.

The storm was to be much worse than the Met Office had predicted. It was sweeping in from the south-west, filling and building as it came. It was not long before the water started coming up over the main deck. Some of the crew went up on to the rig floor to watch the two tugs battle to keep the huge barge head-on into the wind and sea.

Inside the control room, as the light started to fade that afternoon, they checked the weather forecasts again. The Met Office was saying the storm would get steadily worse all evening and start to slacken only at two the next morning. Ten hours to get through before then. They were experienced men, but they were starting to worry.

And then one of the two tow lines snapped.

Everything started to go wrong at once. It was the line on the port side that had gone. Now the rig was being held only by the tug on the starboard side. The rig swung, broadside-on, to the gale and the rising waves. Water started to break over the port side, and into the machine spaces.

Dougie Armstrong, the barge engineer, felt the rig pitch and roll alarmingly under his feet. The noise was unbearable; the high-pitched howl of the wind and the crash of the waves as they hit the side numbed his mind for a moment.

He knew it was serious; but none of them on board knew then the rig was doomed.

The brute strength of the waves tore a container, forty feet long and ten feet high, from its place on the side of the vessel. It had been lashed and chained down; it was even welded into position. But the storm snatched it loose and sent it sliding along the deck. Unknown to the crew, it was smashing along the port side, breaking open vents and punching through bulkheads.

Down below, Billy Mitchell watched with growing alarm as the water started coming into the engine room and the air compressor compartment. He and his mates found plastic sheets to put over the engines and the compressors. The bilge pumps were full on to pump the water out, but they couldn't cope. The water level was rising. As darkness fell outside, the whole rig's crew was called to a meeting in the recreation room.

> 'The storm was to be much worse than the Met Office had predicted. It was sweeping in from the south-west, filling and building as it came'

The rig manager had been in some tricky situations in a working life offshore. He had even been on a drilling rig that had been driven on to the rocks. He knew they were in trouble and wanted to make sure as few lives as possible would be at risk.

As he looked at the men assembled in front of him he was grateful it was only a small crew that manned the rig when it was under tow. Just fifty-one men, including himself, whose lives might depend on the decisions made in the next few minutes.

Briefly, he summed up the situation. The single remaining tug could make no headway against the winds that were already storm force eight and still rising. It hadn't the power, and, anyway, if it put too much of a strain on the line and it broke they would be finished. The weather was getting worse. The rig was shipping water. He was ordering an evacuation of all but the eight most essential personnel. He turned away to the radio room to call ashore for an emergency helicopter airlift.

Billy Mitchell knew he was one of the eight who would have to stay. He still wasn't particularly scared – just fed up, thinking his mates would be snug and warm that night in a pub in Great Yarmouth, and he would be stuck offshore.

Dougie Armstrong was also resigned to staying on board. He would be in charge of the skeleton crew. All they had to do was keep the barge afloat until the weather changed. He did not know then the job had already become impossible.

Stuart Gregg was glad he wasn't going out that night.

The wind was battering the windows of his house. The rain was practically horizontal. A good night for staying in with the television, and the heating turned up high.

He was a helicopter pilot, an experienced one. He had started flying in the army twenty-three years before, and had done 7,000 flying hours in helicopters. It added up to a whole year of his life in the air. Now he was a training captain with Bristow Helicopters, teaching and examining other pilots. But however experienced you are, there are some nights you're happy to stay on the ground, and indoors. He made himself a cup of coffee, and wondered what was for dinner. It was 6.35 pm, and the phone started to ring.

Mike Wood had spent the day ferrying workers to the gas fields close in to the Norfolk coast. The wind had been bad, and had got steadily worse during the afternoon. It was already blowing seventy miles an hour by the time he landed from his last trip. Pilots cultivate understatement. He told them, back at base, he was 'rather pleased' to be finished, and was finishing off his paperwork when the call came through.

Within minutes the two pilots were airborne in a Sikorsky S76A, the workhorse of the North Sea. It was pitch dark, the wind was now nearly eighty miles an hour and gusting even higher. The helicopter was being thrown around like a cork in a fountain.

Stuart Gregg was flying the helicopter from the captain's seat, on the right-hand side of the cockpit. Mike Wood was in the co-pilot's seat on the left. As far as they were concerned this was a 'precautionary evacuation', not a full-scale emergency. As they bucked and swayed in the storm, they reminded each other they were legally bound not to risk themselves and their aircraft beyond normal operating limits. Of course, if lives were at risk, it would be different. But there had been no 'mayday' call. It was all just a precaution.

It didn't look that way, when they broke through the cloud over the rig.

It was visibly down in the water on the port side. The main body of the rig was being thrown up and down by thirty-foot waves, rolling and pitching in the boiling sea. What made it look more dramatic and, from the helicopter crew's point of view, more dangerous, was the rig's enormous legs, which stuck up 400 feet into the air on each corner and were now corkscrewing around in great figures of eight.

Stuart Gregg brought the Sikorsky into the hover, above and slightly to the side of the rig, while they debated whether to try to land. It was, he said, a fine line between taking the risk and everybody saying, 'Well done!' and things going wrong and people saying, 'Why on earth did you do it?'

The situation was way beyond their normal operating limits, but they could see the evacuation was now more than a precaution, it was fast becoming an emergency. They decided they had no choice but to try.

There was another problem. Stuart Gregg was the more experienced of the two, and less tired, but the helicopter had to be landed into the wind, crabbing in from the right. Only Mike Wood, sitting in the left-hand seat, could see where they were going. He would have to do the landing.

It was down to luck and timing. They had to slide between the wildly swinging legs. Then they had to catch the precise moment when the rig was on the top of a wave, and midway through its pitch and roll. If they caught the helideck as it was rising vertically they would crash. It they touched down when the deck was tilting front to back, or side to side, the helicopter would break its undercarriage. Even if they weren't killed, it would probably prevent any other helicopter landing, which, it turned out, would have condemned everybody to death.

They brushed past one of the giant legs as it lunged sideways, and hung for a moment over the helideck, before it rolled away and disappeared, sideways and down underneath them. Mike Wood tried to move the aircraft in time with the pitching and rolling of the rig. They both watched for a moment when everything was horizontal and the rig was at the top of its movement.

It seemed to both of them like hours. Then, for a split second, everything seemed to stop. Stuart Gregg shouted, 'Now!' They both grabbed at the controls and the helicopter hit the deck.

They had landed, not crashed. But now they were in even more danger. The moment they touched the helideck Mike Wood pushed the power down and handed control back to Stuart Gregg who, somehow, had to stop the helicopter sliding off the deck or being thrown straight into the sea. They warned the rig's radio operator they might have to lift off again at any moment.

As the men crawled, one by one, across the netting that had been laid over the helideck, Mike Wood tried to prise open the aircraft's door in the teeth of the gale. The only way he could hold it open was with his left leg, lying sideways across the seat. He managed to keep it ajar long enough for the first ten men to climb aboard.

Stuart Gregg had his hands full. There is no downward force on a helicopter. He was effectively trying to fly it while it was on the deck, tilting the rotor blades into the movement of the rig, as it pitched and rolled. It felt like the very worst kind of fairground ride.

That was certainly what it sounded like to Dale Moon, captain of the second Bristow helicopter, inbound and ten minutes away. Stuart Gregg was trying to brief him on what to expect, but every few seconds all he could hear was 'Whoooooogh!' Like a kid on a roller-coaster, Dale thought. He knew Stuart as a steady,

experienced pilot. It must be tough out there.

Dale W. Moon was an old hand himself, an American who had flown with the US Army in Vietnam and all over the world as a civilian pilot since. This was worse than he could ever remember. The ride out had been bad enough, but now he had broken through the low cloudbase over the rig, and seen what they had to do, he knew it was going to be one of the toughest assignments of his life.

Below him, he could see Stuart Gregg and Mike Wood lifting off. They disappeared into the murk on a heading that would take them to the nearest fixed production platform, the *Sean Papa*.

The rig was now well down by the stern. Some of the decks were awash. The great legs were spinning crazily. But the helideck was still clear of the waves, and Stuart and Mike had proved it could be done.

Dale Moon, and his co-pilot, Roger Williams, edged closer.

They took their time working out how to attempt a landing, but reached the same conclusion as the first crew. Because of the way the rig was lying, broadside to the wind, they, too, would have to land from the left-hand, co-pilot's, side of the helicopter. Roger Williams, a skilled pilot but less experienced than the other three, took the controls and headed towards the tossing deck.

He was close in, fighting the storm and trying to manoeuvre the aircraft through the legs and over the helideck, when he suddenly felt the task was beyond him. Sensing this Dale took back control of the helicopter. It was a tough decision, and a brave one. It wasn't only their lives that were at risk: a botched landing would close off the only escape route for everybody.

The helicopter circled, the pilots wondering what to do. Men's lives were at stake. The only way they could land was if the rig was on his side of the cockpit as they came down. They had to land into the wind. There was only one answer.

He'd have to fly in backwards.

And that's what he did. In the pitch black, in the teeth of an eighty-mile-an-hour gale, with the deck now moving vertically up and down forty feet or more and spinning wildly at the same time, Dale Moon reversed his helicopter towards the landing point as if he was at a summer afternoon flying display.

To the increasingly desperate men below he made it look easy. It was anything but.

For a start, he couldn't see where he was going. He couldn't even keep a sense of balance. The darkness and the storm meant there was no horizon to which he could relate. The sections of the rig he could see kept spinning away from him. He couldn't see the sea, except for a few reflections from the lights on the rig. His senses didn't like it; he could feel he was getting vertigo.

But, somehow, his brain managed to adjust and cope. He levelled off and edged backwards, praying that he would not hit one of the rig's legs; every second waiting for the bang of his tail rotor striking metal. The last thing, he thought, he would ever hear.

But there was no bang. Soon he was over the deck, and trying to time his touchdown for the single moment when the rig was at the top of its swing in the giant waves. He held it for a few moments, screwed up his courage, and dropped it perfectly into place.

He knew then why Stuart Gregg's voice had sounded so odd over the radio. It was the toughest ride he had ever had in his life. The movement was tremendous. He fought to hold the aircraft on the deck, and began to feel sick.

Outside, men were crawling across the helideck towards him. The wind was so fierce it was impossible to stand up. Dale Moon saw one man who tried to walk upright blown right off his feet by the force of the wind, and go rolling across the deck. He scrabbled a handhold in the netting just short of the edge, high over the boiling sea.

The last of the batch of ten men to be evacuated had fought their way on board when there was a new crisis. From his cockpit Dale Moon could see the wind tearing at the long ropes that held the netting on to the helideck. Before he could lift off, the ropes parted and the net hissed back across the deck, under the helicopter. Dale Moon was ninety per cent certain the undercarriage was snagged. But there was no chance, and no time, to get out and disentangle it. He would just have to gamble on breaking free.

He lifted away from the pitching deck, and knew straight away he was caught.

He increased the power. The ropes, snarled in his landing wheels, held the aircraft for a moment – then snapped. He was free.

He set off for the *Sean Papa*, wondering how long his luck was going to hold. If they had tried to take off more quickly the helicopter would have flipped over and crashed on to the deck. So many ways we could have been killed already, he thought.

Behind him the rig's crew were crawling over the helideck trying to fix the net back in place. There were still thirty-one men on board.

Dougie Armstrong, the barge engineer, still thought the rig could be saved. He tried to put the frightened members of the crew with older hands, gave everyone some words of reassurance and set off to see how much damage was being done below. It was bad enough in the control room, where you could barely hear yourself think because of the battering of the waves. With two of the men he went down the stairways to the lower decks.

The engine room was awash. He opened the door to the compressor room. It looked like it was under three or four feet of water, but it was hard to tell because the rig was rolling so much. Through the smashed air vents, he could see a solid wall of green water. He watched it filling up the machine rooms.

Billy Mitchell had rigged up an extra welding pump to help the bilge pumps trying to keep the water level down on the port side of the rig. The weight of it was pulling the whole structure over. He could feel how much more slowly it was righting itself now after the waves hit it. The pumps could not keep up. The water level was still rising.

Worse, the water was getting into the rig's electrical systems. He switched the power off to the galley, the rig floor, the drilling equipment – everywhere it was not vitally necessary.

They had to find out where the water was coming in. Billy took two men, a toolpusher and a mechanic, and went up on deck.

What he saw made the hair ripple on the back of his neck. The rig was lying in a trough in the sea with a huge wave, fifty feet high, hanging over it – solid green in the rig's lights and hissing with foam. He had never seen waves so big.

He realized it would be suicidal to try to launch a lifeboat in seas like this. For the first time, Billy Mitchell wondered if he was going to survive the night.

It was dangerous enough just being on deck. The three men roped themselves to fixed points along the side to inspect the outer air ducts. The ones they could see were closed. They decided the water must be getting in through damage below that they could not see. It was a frightening thought, water pouring in where they could do nothing about it.

Back down in the engine room, Billy found the situation was getting worse. The manager came down and handed out the survival equipment, rubberized orange suits that would keep you alive a few extra minutes in the freezing water. Fat lot of good this will do, Billy thought, as he put one on. They all knew it was only a gesture.

Every few seconds now the water was bursting into the engine room. Each time it was like a forty-five-gallon drum being emptied all over them. Billy remembered old submarine movies. That was his special nightmare; the bulkhead door swinging shut and trapping them in a compartment that was filling up with water.

'Through the smashed air vents, he could see a solid wall of green water. He watched it filling up the machine rooms'

Dougie Armstrong was standing by the main transformers when a gush of water cascaded all over them. There was a lot of voltage there. He waited for the bang, but it didn't happen. He still had faith in the strength of the rig. He still felt it would survive the night, and his job was to make sure it did.

He went back to the control room and what he found there shook his faith severely. It wasn't just the instruments, which showed the rig pitching and rolling way beyond its official limitations. It was the feel of the whole structure. Each time it dipped, sideways, into the trough, it seemed more reluctant to come up again. It just hung there. People were saying to each other, 'What the hell's going on?' They were scared. By now, even Dougie Armstrong was scared.

It was now clear to everyone that it was a full-scale emergency. The winds and tides had swept the rig seven miles from its original position. An RAF Nimrod had been scrambled from Kinloss in Scotland to act as an airborne radar and communications base. RAF Sea King air–sea rescue helicopters had arrived over the rig. But there was little they could do. Three times they had tried to land, but the great yellow helicopters were too big, and not manoeuvrable enough. As a last resort they could try winching people off; but the chances were they would be battered to death by the thrashing legs of the rig.

Tonight, they were spectators. It was up to the two Bristow helicopters. It was them, or nothing.

They had both done another trip. Stuart Gregg had flown ten men to the *Sean Papa*, Dale Moon ten more back to base in Great Yarmouth.

Eleven men left on board now, and at this stage they were still planning to leave eight behind to try to save the rig.

Stuart Gregg and Mike Wood brought their helicopter in for the last time. The weather was so bad their radar was useless. They were vectored on to the rig by the RAF Nimrod, circling overhead at 30,000 feet. Each landing had been more difficult than the last and this would be the worst of all. Mike Wood edged forward.

They were 150 feet above the sea, and 200 yards from the rig, when it suddenly disappeared. All the lights went out. The vast structure, gone, in a fraction of a second.

Both pilots felt they had jumped two inches out of their seats with the shock. In the sudden darkness, blinded by the loss of the lights, they slowly backed away and tried to work out what had happened.

Down in the rig, all was darkness. The hum and hiss and clank of machinery, all the mechanical noises that formed a background to life offshore, had stopped. All they could hear now was the roaring of the sea, the thrashing of the waves as they crashed on to the control room.

Moments before, the rig had given a great heave; lurched so wildly nobody on board thought it would come back. It was easy enough to work out what had happened; the main transformers must have blown up. The emergency generators had not come on, but that was probably because they were under water by now. Nobody was volunteering to go down five decks to check.

There was now no question of anybody staying on board. The radio operator switched to his emergency set and started broadcasting 'Mayday', an appeal for complete evacuation.

'Each landing had been more difficult than the last and this would be the worst of all'

Stuart Gregg and Mike Wood were circling some distance from the last place they'd seen the rig, trying to get their night vision back. Gradually, they could make out the ghostly impression of the superstructure. They could feel it was there, rather than see it. They flew back towards it again.

Below them some of the remaining crew had scrambled out of the control room, up three or four steps on to the muster deck. They waited there, in the shelter of some pipes, praying for a sight of the helicopter lights.

Huge seas were now sweeping over the rig. At one point Billy Mitchell thought he saw the aircraft's lights and realized

with a shock he was looking at a tug, thrown way above what he thought should be the horizon by a giant wave.

Dougie Armstrong was trying to feel lucky. It *had* been a stroke of good fortune, the electricity failing when it did. A few minutes later and the last helicopter would have gone. He and his skeleton crew would have had no chance. Not, he thought, that their chances were that good now.

All Stuart Gregg and Mike Wood had to guide them was the landing light on the underside of the helicopter. They made their approach even more slowly than on the previous two landings, moving forward a few yards and then stopping to make sure the helicopter was stable. The rig reared up underneath them and skidded back down into a trough in the waves. On the previous occasions they had had to wait, sweating, on the movements of the rig coming together to let them land. This time they struck lucky. At precisely the moment they reached the centre of the helideck, it rose up to meet them and Mike Wood just plopped it down.

Billy Mitchell, knowing his survival depended on the landing, thought it was brilliant, like someone putting a frying pan on a stove.

The last eleven men made it through the roaring gale to the helideck in stages. Out of the control room, then across the muster deck to be grabbed by a man wedged into the shelter of the jet fuel tanks. Up the cantilevered steps on to the helideck, where another man was tied down ready to hold the others against the force of the wind. Then down, hand over hand, across the netting towards the lights of the helicopter.

Dougie Armstrong was the last to leave. For reasons he still cannot explain, he went back down the companionway and unplugged his television set. Then he went back on top and hauled himself across the helideck, and was pulled into the aircraft.

In the cockpit, Stuart Gregg was fighting to hold the helicopter on to the deck, and Mike Wood was counting heads. There were eleven men to rescue, and eleven seats available in the rear of the aircraft (the twelfth carried a spare liferaft). Every seat ought to be full.

But one was empty.

The pilots were desperate to go. Any moment the helicopter could be thrown bodily off the deck, or slide off at the sort of angle that would make it impossible for the rotor blades to get any lift before it hit the sea. But they knew there would be no other chance; anybody they left behind would die.

Three times Mike Wood counted heads. Ten, only ten, for God's sake. The helicopter jerked sideways, and Stuart Gregg only just stopped it in time.

Mike Wood started to count heads a fourth time. Then, to his unimaginable relief, he saw an extra head rise up out of the back row. One of the last aboard had been too exhausted to find a seat and had just been dragged on to the laps of his colleagues.

Stuart Gregg pushed the controls right and forward and, slowly, the helicopter staggered into the air. Some of the rig's crew started to cry.

Ten minutes later, as the helicopter bucked and heaved in the turbulence on its way to Great Yarmouth, the message came through that the rig had sunk.

It was as close as that.

The Bristow helicopter pilots who helped foil the widowmaker (left to right) Captains Wood, Gregg, Moon and Williams

For their part in the rescue, Captain Stuart Gregg and Captain Mike Wood were awarded the Queen's Gallantry Medal, for 'conspicuous gallantry and devotion to duty' in rescuing the crew of the rig, at considerable risk to their own safety.

CHAPTER 12
All in a Day's Work

999 'Somewhere over Cardiff a complete novice was alone at the controls of an aircraft'

'Mayday! Mayday!'

The international distress call is known and recognized all over the world. Everybody stops when they hear it. Someone, somewhere, is in mortal danger.

The effect in the control tower at Cardiff airport that sunlit afternoon in late March was electrifying. Until then, it had all been normal, routine, almost dull. But that call started the most extraordinary half-hour in the airport's history. The odds against the caller surviving were later estimated by the Civil Aviation Authority to be several thousand to one. Statistically, he was already as good as dead.

'This is Cardiff, Mayday. Go ahead.'

John Hibbard was the only controller in the darkened approach room. Half of his mind was on his training in emergency procedures, the other half was wondering who it was, and what sort of mess they were in. He knew most of the qualified pilots in South Wales, but did not recognize this voice.

'Yeah. I've just gone up with Les in, er, Golf Alpha Yankee Delta Golf.'

A terrible thought was forming in John Hibbard's mind as he responded automatically.

'Delta Golf, Roger. Go ahead.'

'I think he's had a heart attack, and I haven't a bloody clue what to do!'

For a few seconds everybody listening in to the frequency thought it must be a student pilot, with a sick instructor. That would have been bad enough. But the next exchange showed it was much, much worse.

'Delta Golf, Roger. Your present position?'

'Er . . . er . . . I haven't got a clue. I don't even know how to read the dials!'

Somewhere over Cardiff a complete novice was alone at the controls of an aircraft. Nobody could rescue him. His life was in his own hands. One clumsy move, one wrong decision and he was dead. He shouldn't have had a chance.

In fact, it was only the second time in his life that Alan Anderson had ever been in a plane. He hated heights. He didn't even like going up a ladder, if he could help it.

His girlfriend Alison's father, Les Rhodes, was always trying to get him to go up in the little plane he kept at Cardiff airport. Alan kept saying, 'One day.' That evening, he had simply run out of excuses.

He had only just got back to Alison's house from work, when Les had called round.

'Where is he then? Is he coming for a bumble?' That was what he called his trips in the little Rallye Minerva, which buzzed like a bee over the South Wales valleys.

He was sixty-three, and only six months away from retirement. But he was full of energy and felt fit. His regular medical check, only a fortnight before, had been clear.

In any case, he never worried about flying. Several times he had told Alan that was the way he wanted to go: 'The best way I could die is in the plane,' he would say. 'I'd go out with a God Almighty bang.'

Half an hour later they were airborne, and circling the airport. Les had decided to head west along the coast, maybe land in Swansea for tea. It was a beautifully clear evening and Les was obviously a confident pilot. Alan began to relax and enjoy himself.

It was twenty minutes into the flight when Les had a massive heart attack, which killed him instantly.

'He pressed the button to call Air Traffic Control . . . then he tried to remember the word they used in the movies when people were in trouble'

Alan did not see it happen. He heard no noise. He was looking straight ahead, when the plane lurched and started to fall out of the sky in a long, right-hand spiral.

At first he thought it was a joke. Les liked practical jokes; it would be absolutely typical to pretend the plane was in trouble if he thought Alan was getting a bit cocky.

Alan's head was dragged back by the accelerating 'G' forces. He glanced sideways and saw Les slumped forward, and he began to realize something was very wrong. He reached forward for the control column.

It must have been luck. He had no idea how he got the aircraft to straighten out. As soon as it was level, he stretched across and reached under Les's jacket. He could not feel a heartbeat. Alan was all alone, and very scared.

He pressed the button to call Air Traffic Control, the way he had watched Les do a few minutes before. Then he tried to remember the word they used in the movies when people were in trouble.

Colin Eaton was sitting in the restaurant in the terminal building when the tannoy went off. He was the other controller on duty in the approach room that afternoon. He was on his break, sipping his coffee and watching a giant Lockheed TriStar circling a beacon above the airport, when the loudspeaker broke into life and ordered him to report to the control tower, immediately.

Such a thing had never happened before, that he could remember. He left his coffee, ran down the stairs and took the 400 yards to the tower at a sprint.

'You are not going to believe this.' John Hibbard could barely believe it himself.

'The pilot's dead, the passenger's trying to fly it, but hasn't got the remotest idea how.'

He briefed Colin as quickly as he could and handed over responsibility for handling the emergency. He would have his hands full keeping all the other aircraft clear until Alan Anderson came down. In one piece, or, as seemed infinitely more likely, in several.

'Delta Golf. Just to confirm. There are two on board and the pilot has had a heart attack, you suspect, and you cannot fly the aircraft.'

'Yeah. That's affirmative.'

The first thing was to find out where the plane was, and which way it was going.

'Delta Golf, Roger. Do you know, er, can you look down and see your position? Are you over the water or the coast?'

Alan quickly looked out of the side of the cockpit: 'Over the coast at the moment.'

'Delta Golf Mayday. Can you look at the dials ahead of you and tell what heading you are on? Look at the compass . . . see what it's pointing at . . . see what the needles are pointing at.'

'Yeah. It says number 12 next to the E.'

Dear God, Colin thought. But he had to try to sound confident for the lad's sake.

'That's fine. You're on a south-easterly heading, directly back towards the airport. How is the pilot now?'

Alan felt him again. 'Yeah. He's still the same. He's cold. Oh, shit, what do I do now?'

Colin Eaton could hear the fear in Alan's voice. He had to stop it turning into panic. He tried to sound calm and professional, as if this was something that was almost routine.

'Delta Golf, Roger. Remain on this frequency. I'll call you back as soon as I can. Just continue on the present heading for the time being.'

Bloody hell, he thought. We'll have to talk him down from here. No compass, no giro, he can't read the instruments. He can barely steer it, let alone do a landing.

Not for the first time, Colin was grateful for the flight training he was given as part of his job. Britain is the only country that insists its air traffic controllers do some flying themselves. Colin knew what it was like in the cockpit.

'Delta Golf. Can you see what your present altitude is – see how high you are?'

'Yeah. Whereabout is that on the dials then?'

'See if you can see something that says A-L-T. Altitude.'

Alan scanned the dials in front of him. 'Yeah, I can see that. Er, the little hand's just below, or just about the two. The other's just below the seven.'

Two and a half thousand feet. He was low, but there was a few minutes' breathing space if he could keep it steady, and not tip it into a spin.

At that point another voice broke onto the frequency. Robert Legg was an instructor flying Charlie Echo out to the west of the airport that evening. At first he had thought the mayday was a joke. But now he could hear the distress in the man's voice. He reckoned he was about five miles from the other aircraft. He called up and offered to help.

Colin Eaton had been planning to call in a flying instructor to the control room. This was better, he thought; manna from heaven. He vectored the instructor towards his new pupil, and quietly crossed his fingers.

'Golf Alpha Yankee Delta Golf. This is the air traffic controller speaking to you. For your information, sir, there is an aircraft which is about four miles to the west of you. He is rapidly approaching you now to draw alongside, and then the pilot of that aircraft will be speaking to you on this frequency.'

'OK. I've never done this before, mind.'

Robert Legg had flown with many different people of all standards. Hardly any would have been capable of taking control of an aircraft and keeping calm with so little experience. He couldn't think of one who would be able to land it. He must keep it simple, he thought.

'Delta Golf, this is Charlie Echo, can you hear me?'

'Yeah, how much longer are we going to be?'

'I'll get you down as quickly as possible. If you look to your right, just behind your wing, you may see my aircraft.'

'I can see you. Thank God you're there!'

For a split second Alan felt an overwhelming sense of relief. It was going to be all right. He did not quite know what would happen now, but in the movies the canopy of the other plane would open and they would drop a pilot into his cockpit to fly him home.

It wasn't going to be that easy.

Quietly, calmly, Robert Legg explained that Alan was going to have to land it himself. He was going to have to follow his instructions absolutely.

Alan no longer felt so lonely. He felt now he would have some company when he died.

999 'If you look to your right, just behind your wing, you may see my aircraft'

'OK. I would like you to take the throttle and pull it out until the RPM drops down to about twenty-three hundred.'

'Yeah. Which one's the throttle?'

'There should be a black lever in the centre of the panel, in between the two control columns . . . Pull back slightly on the control column to raise the nose. That's good. OK, don't pull back too far, ease forward on the controls. That's fine. Let the aircraft fly itself.'

'I wish it would!'

The two had been flying in formation. Then, suddenly, Alan disappeared.

He had pulled the throttle back too far and his aircraft fell away under Robert Legg's wing. For a moment, the instructor panicked. If Alan jerked back on the control column to regain height he would come back up under his plane, and they would both be dead. He peeled steeply away to the left until he could see where Alan had gone. This was going to be even more difficult than he'd thought.

He told himself again he must keep it simple. Little bits of information. Simple step-by-step instructions. He must not over-load him. If he pushed him too far he would be finished.

Alan called him up: 'I tell you, I have never been so scared in my life.'

'Try to relax, as much as you can. You're doing very well.'

Down in the darkened approach room in the control tower, Colin Eaton was feeling helpless. He had seen tragedies, he had seen pilots killed, but never before had he felt there was nothing, absolutely nothing, he could do. It was up to the two of them.

In many ways they were lucky that evening. The weather was unusually clear. There was practically no wind, not even the usual sea breezes that normally sprang up at that time of day, blowing in from the Bristol Channel. Their course had brought them over the airfield, with the sun setting behind them. Alan was desperate to get down.

'We're going down, are we?'

'We will be shortly. I want you to maintain your altitude at this time. Maintain your altitude.'

'I can see the runway!'

Robert Legg had brought Alan round in a long sweeping approach. But as they began the descent, losing speed and height over the rooftops, he knew this was by far the most dangerous part of the operation. Alan had survived until now mainly by luck. His chances of surviving the next five minutes were very small indeed.

Robert had explained it to every pupil he had trained. 'Basically,' he'd say, 'the aim is to fly the aircraft as slowly as is safely possible. But the margins are narrow. Reduce throttle too much, pull back on the control column too far, and the aircraft will suddenly stall, and fall out of the sky.'

Colin Eaton had seen experienced pilots kill themselves by getting it slightly wrong on the approach to the runway. The blinds were still down in the approach room, but he was getting progress reports from the tower controller who dealt with movements around the airport from the room above him.

There was a terrible moment as Alan's plane came round the downwind end of the circuit and the tower lost sight of him. They all braced themselves for the bang and the smoke. But Alan completed the circuit and came back into sight, heading for the runway.

Robert Legg's voice was there, all the time, in his headphones.

'OK. Should be coming round on your left now. I want you to keep the aircraft turning until you're pointing towards the runway. Get it as close to the centre line as you can.

'OK. I'd like you to slightly reduce the throttle – and I mean only slightly.

'OK. Hold the wings level. Now let's get on to the centre line. Come over to the right a little.

'OK. I'd like you to pull back very gently on the control column. *Very* gently indeed . . . hold that position there.'

Robert Legg had kept it as simple as he possibly could. He hadn't mentioned the flaps that make the wings bigger, and help the plane to land more slowly. The runway at Cardiff was built for jet airliners. It was around 2,500 yards long, big enough to take the risk of a fast landing.

It didn't look that big to Alan Anderson. From a distance it had looked far too tiny to put a plane down on. As he came down towards it, it was getting bigger – but how did he stop it when he hit the runway? Where were the brakes, for Christ's sake? He was convinced that, even if he managed to land, he would go straight across the runway and off the other side.

'Alan had survived until now mainly by luck. His chances of surviving the next five minutes were very small indeed'

'From a distance it had looked far too tiny to put a plane down on'

But, all the time, the voice in his ear.

'Reduce the throttle . . . Pull the throttle slightly towards you . . . Try to put the aircraft on to the tarmac . . . come slightly to the left . . . close the throttle . . . pull the throttle all the way towards you now and pull gently on the control column . . . close the throttle . . . hold it there . . . pull gently back on the control column and hold it there . . . hold it, hold it, hold it!'

The aircraft staggered a moment, seemed to collect itself, and hit the tarmac.

Not for a moment had Robert Legg thought he would land without crashing. When he realized Alan was down, and both he and his aircraft were in one piece, he felt a surge of elation at what he had done.

'Hold the control column back. Relax.'

'I can't find the brakes.'

'OK. On the rudder pedals. On top of the rudder pedals you'll find the brakes.'

The calm professionalism in the control tower gave way for a moment. They had rushed to the blinds to see the landing for themselves. When they saw him touch the runway they started cheering.

'I'm down,' Alan shouted. 'Thank God!'

'You're welcome,' said Robert Legg, as he turned his aircraft away to bring it in to land. 'It's all in a day's work.'

Alan Anderson was taken to hospital suffering from shock. There was nothing anybody could do for Les Rhodes.

Alan married Les's daughter and is talking about taking flying lessons. He says he thinks he's got an aptitude for being a pilot. They went on holiday to Portugal recently in a big airliner, but it wasn't quite the same.

Alan Anderson (left) with his emergency flying instructor Robert Legg

Robert Legg draws a more philosophical lesson from what happened that day. It's made him realize, he says, that nothing is impossible in life. If he hadn't taken the responsibility, if Alan hadn't taken the controls and followed the instructions, they could not have achieved what they did and – even though it was against all the odds – achieved a happy ending.

CHAPTER 13

The Chase

They decided later it was the rain that was really to blame.

One moment young Gavin Hall was running up the hill in the spring sunshine. The next, the earth had opened up and swallowed him. He was in total darkness, twenty feet underground; his head was jammed in a crevice; his body was swinging over a chasm that was close to bottomless.

In the hours that followed he could have died at any moment, along with several of those who came to rescue him. The chances of his survival were never good.

The odds were always on tragedy.

'Everybody knew the odds were still against them'

That Sunday had dawned cloudless and bright, to everybody's relief. For two and a half days the rain in the Midlands had been relentless. Roads had been flooded, some rivers had burst their banks, children had been kept indoors.

As he looked out of the window, Barry Bolton was particularly thankful. Another day cooped up in a house full of kids would have been unbearable. As well as his own four children, their friend, Dawn Hall, had dropped off her five-year-old son Gavin the previous night.

She was coming round later to help his wife cook a big Sunday lunch for them all. Before then, there would be plenty of time to get all the children some fresh air, and wear them out. That way, he thought, they might get some peace in the afternoon. He knew just the place to take them.

Cannock Chase spreads across a dozen square miles of the county of Staffordshire. Long ago it was a hunting forest. Now, the broad stretch of wooded hills and rugged moorland is designated an 'area of outstanding natural beauty', and attracts a million visitors a year.

There were many who went there that morning. Only locals like Barry Bolton know that beneath the Chase is a honeycomb of old workings from centuries of coal mining. What nobody knew then was that the days of heavy rain had made the ground above those workings unstable, opening up cracks in the surface of the ground that were almost impossible to see.

Barry Bolton had done all he could to tire the boys out. Leaving Barry junior at home, he had taken the others, and his dog Smoky, to a stretch of common to play football. When that got too crowded, he had taken them further on to the Chase for another game in a valley that was known to locals as Seven Springs. Their energy was amazing; despite all the exercise, they were still going strong.

While they were playing, he remembered that this was the place where the local football team, Stafford Rangers, came to train. They built up their stamina by running up and down the sides of the valley. He looked at the kids, still racing around. That should fix them.

His two older boys went first. Wesley, who was eleven, followed by Leslie, nine, raced up the path that snaked through the trees and bracken. They branched left at a fork in the path, and emerged, panting hard, at the top.

Gavin was next. He took the right fork, but seemed to think better of it, and left the path to cut back through the bracken. At the bottom of the hill, Barry Bolton turned away for a moment to pick up his youngest son, Christopher. When he turned back, Gavin had disappeared.

'Gavin, where are you Gav?'

They just could not work out where he had gone. Barry kept shouting from the bottom of the valley. He called up to his boys at the top to see if they could see him. But there was no sign at all. Gavin had disappeared into thin air.

Barry was not particularly worried at first. He thought Gavin must be playing, lying under the bracken to wind everybody up. Smoky would soon put a stop to that. He slipped off his lead and watched the dog run off up the hill. Smoky was an odd-looking dog, a collie–spaniel cross with a wall eye, nobody's idea of a thoroughbred. But he had a keen nose; he had been trained to the gun by a gamekeeper friend. Following Gavin's trail should have been no problem at all. But, two-thirds of the way up the hill, the dog stopped and ran around in a circle. He was barking at a bush that, even from where he was standing, Barry could see was too small to hide the boy.

Rabbits, thought Barry, as he followed up the hill, cursing Smoky at the top of his voice. When he got nearer he even aimed a kick at the dog, he was so angry with him.

It was only when he stopped swearing that he heard a faint voice coming out from under the bracken. At first, it did look like a rabbit hole. But when he pushed the bracken aside he saw it was bigger than that.

He shouted, 'Gavin, where are you?'

There was a moment's pause, then a shaky voice replied, 'Down here. I'm down here.'

'Wave your arms around, Gavin. I can't see you.'

Down in the blackness, Barry saw a flicker, as Gavin's fingertips flashed through a stray beam of light. When his eyes adjusted to the darkness, Barry could see what had happened. Gavin had fallen through a hole only about eighteen inches wide, and now seemed to be trapped fifteen to twenty feet down. He could only see the top of his head. He was obviously trapped but, from where he was standing, Barry could not see how.

In fact, Gavin's head was tightly jammed into a crevice, and that was what had saved him. The hole stretched far below where he was hanging. It was certainly several hundred feet deep, but nobody ever established how far down it went. If it had not been for his head being caught Gavin would have died there and then, and his body would never have been found.

Trying hard to keep his voice steady, Barry told Gavin not to worry while he thought desperately about what to do. He sent one of his boys for the tow-rope he kept in his car. If this works, he thought, we'll all be home for lunch.

He tied one end of the rope to a tree with Smoky's lead. He threw the other down the hole to Gavin and started pulling. But, however hard he tried, he couldn't shift him.

Barry started to panic. He needed help, and quickly. He sent one of the older lads off to the Rangers' station to raise the alarm.

Leading Fireman Bernard Gidman was bored. He was a big man in his early forties, a bit of a character. He liked to be busy, and relished the excitement that went with the job. So far, though, it had been a dull day. He and his mate had been sent off in their emergency tender down the M6 motorway to deal with a car that was overheating. But by the time they got there the fire in the engine was out. A wasted trip, like so many of them.

On the way back they began to pick up stray messages on the vehicle's radio. Bernard had noticed before how the police radio broke into the fire service's transmissions at several points on the motorway. Now, near junction 13, they began to hear the police control room talking about a boy trapped at Seven Springs.

Bernard turned to his mate, who was driving. 'Put a spurt on,' he said. 'That's only ten miles from here. They're bound to send us.'

He was right. Two minutes later the controllers at the Staffordshire Fire Headquarters at Stone called them up, gave them a few, sparse details, and told them to hurry.

That's all very well, Bernard grumbled a few minutes later, as he glared out of the fire tender's windscreen. Those people in headquarters just sit in their air-conditioned control room playing with their computer screens; they didn't have to cope with the traffic. The roads that day were packed with people who had turned out to watch the Stafford Marathon. Bernard was just thinking they would never get through, when a police motorcyclist picked them up, carved a way through the crowds and got them to the bottom of the Seven Springs valley less than ten minutes later.

Bernard did not know what to expect. As he ran, breathing heavily, up the one-in-three incline all he could see ahead of him was a group of people just staring at the ground. It was only when he reached them, and Barry Bolton pointed to the hole, that he realized how difficult the rescue was going to be.

Gavin had already been down there half an hour. Bernard yelled down to him, but there was no reply. For a few moments he was convinced the rescue was over before it had begun. We've lost him, he thought.

They all shouted, and began to hear a frightened whimpering from beneath their feet. He was still alive, but his situation was getting more and more desperate.

The ground round the lip of the hole was starting to disintegrate. It was a mixture of sand and gravel and bits of it were crumbling away. Bernard realized that if he did not do something very quickly the hole would collapse and Gavin would be buried alive.

But what?

All he had with him was a couple of ropes he had brought up from the emergency tender. Bernard looked around desperately for something, anything, to push into the hole.

There was only one thing he could do. Tying a rope round his waist, he called over two police motorcyclists who had just arrived and told them what to do. They picked him up, lifted him over and wedged him in it, like a cork in the top of a bottle.

It was not exactly orthodox, but, for the moment he had saved Gavin's life.

Sod's Law was working overtime that day. Bernard's boss, Deputy Chief Fire Officer Robin Richards, had been debating whether to take his wife to the pub or mow the lawn when the call had come through. They said it was urgent, but he still took the time to change into his uniform. It helped people to know who was in charge.

He'd had a clear run so far but, just as he was coming into the village of Great Haywood, just when he needed to clear the traffic, the blue light on top of his official white Ford Sierra stopped working. He did his best, flashing his lights, sounding his horn, but the road to Seven Springs was full of motorists who started by being unco-operative, and ended up very angry indeed.

When Robin Richards reached the hillside to take charge, the rescue services were gathering in strength, but there was still no plan for getting Gavin out. At least they had now brought up air bags, which they pushed into the hole on either side of Bernard Gidman, so he could extricate himself without the hole immediately caving in. The fire service controllers had tracked down some planks at a building site behind the Territorial Army centre in Stafford, and they were being brought to shore up the hole. For the time being, they thought they could keep it open but it was obviously unstable. Robin Richards had trained as a geologist and could see what the problems were. He knew they would not have long. He also knew there would be no chance of getting the boy out, the way he had fallen in.

By now they had a clearer idea of Gavin's situation. He was a skinny boy and had gone straight down until he had been trapped by his head, the widest part of his body. What they didn't know was what condition he was in. Bernard Gidman had been talking to him, telling him over and over again, 'Don't worry, Gavin. We'll have you out for tea.' But he was not getting much response.

A doctor from the local hospital was worried about broken bones, about shock, hypothermia and dehydration. He was only five. The doctor laid it firmly on the line: 'If you don't get him out soon, he'll die.'

And there was another worry for Robin Richards. They were beginning to realize how deep the hole went. Their torches showed the hole went down far below Gavin; even the most powerful beam petered out in the darkness before it showed any sign of the bottom. They could not tell how firmly he was held. At any moment, he might slip away from them altogether.

Robin Richards knew his firemen were tough, experienced and adaptable. But this was a job for experts at working in narrow tunnels, underground. A job for miners. Thank God they were on their way.

The emergency controllers had made two other calls after they had sent the fire engines and the police up to Seven Springs. One set off Peter Hurley's bleeper, ordering him to report to the fire station at Rugeley. He was a part-timer, a 'retained' fireman, and part of the duty crew that weekend. As chance would have it, he was already there, washing his car.

The computer message from fire headquarters at Stone was waiting in the muster bay. He waited for the first six volunteers to arrive – a full crew for the fire engine – not knowing then it was the expertise of his full-time job that would be needed, not his skills as a weekend firefighter. Peter Hurley was a maintenance engineer for British Coal.

Another call set off Mick Cape's pager as he was washing in his bathroom. He was duty officer for the mine rescue station at Hednesford. He had once been a miner himself, but for the last twelve years his job had been to go into pits after an accident and pull miners out.

His thoughts, as he headed for Seven Springs with his boss, Cliff Lewis, and the rest of the team in their van, were on the only other time he had been called upon to rescue a boy, rather than a man. It had taken two and a half days to pump out the shaft where he was trapped, and they had known for a long time the boy would be dead. It had been years before, but it was not something you forget.

The mine rescue team carried a special piece of equipment with them, a combination microphone and loudspeaker, and the first thing they did when they got to the site was to lower it down the hole. It meant they could both talk to Gavin and hear him. By now he was a very frightened little boy and his crying was audible to everybody on the hillside.

The priority was to find a way to reach him. Robin Richards and the mine rescue superintendent, Cliff Lewis, had both noticed other small holes and depressions along the contour line nearby. It was Cliff Lewis, with his mining experience, who realized what they meant. It was not a hole that Gavin had fallen down, but a long fissure. Below the topsoil, he reckoned the rock itself had split along a crack dozens of yards in either direction. He picked a spot fifteen yards away and slightly downhill from where Gavin had fallen, and they started digging. Almost at once, the soil fell away and the fissure appeared beneath them.

The plan was simple. They would have to widen the crack, then work their way along the fissure and down to where Gavin was trapped. It was risky. The ground could close up as rapidly as it had broken open. But there was no other option available. They called for volunteers.

Three were chosen. Mick Cape was the first. He was the obvious choice: a miner, a rescue expert, and – most important that day – he was the smallest person there. He was short, just 5ft 7in, and only 9½ stone, thanks to all the training he did with the local tug-of-war team at Rugeley Power Station.

Peter Hurley volunteered. He had been brought up under-ground, he said. It was his natural environment.

Bernard Gidman insisted on being in the team, too. He might not be at home in a tunnel under the hill, but he had established

contact and a measure of trust with Gavin. He was not going to be left behind.

It was now nearly one o'clock. Gavin had been trapped for an hour and a half and nobody knew how long he could last. They called for extra equipment and started widening the hole to make it into a relief shaft. Everybody knew the odds were still against them.

Back at the Boltons' house Gavin's mother, Dawn, and Hazel Bolton were getting worried. The lunch was nearly ready, the meat was already overdone, and there was still no sign of Barry or the children. Out of the corner of her eye Dawn saw a police car draw up outside. She recognized the policeman who came to the door. Even before he said it was bad news, she had read the expression on his face.

She wanted to go up to Cannock Chase, but the police had other ideas. Things were not going well up there; the boy's chances of getting out alive were not good. The last thing they wanted was

'They picked a spot fifteen yards away slightly downhill from where Gavin had fallen, and they started digging. Almost at once, the soil fell away and the fissure appeared beneath them'

a hysterical mother getting in the way. They took her instead to Stafford police station, promising to keep her totally informed about what was happening. On the way there, all that Dawn could think about was that Gavin was going to die. How had she been with him recently? Had she shouted at him? What would be his last memories of her?

Up on the hill, they had at last widened the entrance hole to the relief shaft, and shored it up as best they could to stop it caving in. Mick Cape strapped a harness on, made sure the lines to the surface were clear, and squeezed, head first, into the hole. It was only about ten inches wide.

Part of him was conscious of the dangers. The trickle of soil on his back showed how unstable the ground was above him. Although he was working his way diagonally down a narrow crack in the rock he was sure it widened as it got deeper – 'bottled out' as miners say. At any moment there was the chance he would fall into the deep, suffocating darkness where nobody would reach him. But he could hear Gavin moaning somewhere ahead. He tried to focus on the little boy, and forget everything else. Chipping at the rock, twisting and shoving his body through the gaps, he inched forward towards the noise.

'He tried to focus on the little boy, and forget everything else. Chipping at the rock, twisting and shoving his body through the gaps, he inched forward towards the noise'

On the surface, Robin Richards was adding up all the things that could go wrong, painfully aware he was the man in charge, the man who would be held responsible. He was no miner, but he knew the risks the rescuers had to run. The line round Mick Cape, he thought, would only show them where to find his body if anything happened. They'd set up a briefing every twenty minutes, to monitor progress, and it was agonizingly slow. They could all hear Gavin through the loudspeaker they had set up. It was bad enough when he was crying, but the long silences were worse. He had been down there three hours. In those cold conditions, in shock, maybe injured, no food and drink, he would not survive for long. Looking over his shoulder, Robin could see where the press and TV cameras were waiting. It must be a slow news day, he thought. There's dozens of them. What will they say if we don't get him out alive?

In the fissure, Mick Cape had been relieved by Peter Hurley. It was so cramped, it was such strenuous work to bore their way down through the fissure, they could only do it a few minutes at a time. Just to move a yard forward meant long hacking at the sandstone, and twisting round through 360 degrees. They could see Gavin's body now in the gloom. All Peter could think of was how like his son Elliot he was. Same age, similar build. It could have been his own son down there. As he worked, he kept talking to Gavin. It was partly reassurance, partly to keep him awake. He knew that once he lapsed into unconsciousness, he wouldn't last long.

It was Bernard Gidman who did most to keep Gavin's spirits up when he took his turn in the shaft. He had been the first of the rescuers to speak to Gavin and when he went down into the fissure he talked to him quietly, telling him how the operation was going, and promising him they would get him out alive, but it might take time. Gavin whimpered a lot, but seemed to understand. Every so often he would cry out for his mother.

Dawn was still at the police station, but getting more and more frustrated. Every few minutes a policeman would come and talk to her, but he had very little news. Dawn kept saying she wanted to go up to the Chase, but the police were still reluctant. Eventually, after she had threatened to call a taxi and go up on her own, they backed down.

The police had two worries. They did not want Dawn to hear Gavin's crying, particularly as it was now coming over a loudspeaker from the microphone they had dropped near him. And they were also concerned that if Gavin heard his mother he might struggle and fall further into the hole, beyond their reach.

In the end, Dawn allowed herself to be persuaded it was better to stay in a police car, at the bottom of the hill up to Seven Springs. It was just as well. The rescue was going badly. It was now four o'clock in the afternoon. Gavin's crying had lowered the morale of the rescue team. Now the silences were getting longer. Robin Richards, in charge on the hillside, thought the operation was now bound to fail; they would never get him out in time.

But somewhere below Robin Richards's feet, Mick Cape had taken over again and had cut and squirmed his way close to Gavin. He could clearly see Gavin's legs hanging down over the chasm, but his head and the upper part of his body were covered in dirt that had fallen on him. He could hear the effect it was having on his breathing, and reckoned there was a danger he could suffocate.

Mick Cape passed the word back for something to scrape off the dirt. At first they sent down a stick and he poked it carefully round the boy's head until he could see his hair sticking out the top. Then they sent down a little vacuum cleaner. Gently, Mick Cape cleared the debris away from Gavin's eyes, which had been tightly shut, and a moment later the mask of dirt covering his face fell away.

He opened his eyes, the first sign of life for several minutes. He tried to move but he was still held fast by the upper part of his body, and particularly his head. That was jammed so tightly into the crevice he could not move it any direction at all.

Mick Cape felt Gavin's body all over, looking for broken bones. His arm was trapped behind his back, but after several minutes wriggling and pulling, Mick Cape managed to release it. He called for a line and tied it to Gavin's arm, in case he slipped further down the crevice.

Bernard had come up behind Mick, and between them they decided to see if they could tug him free. Mick took hold of Gavin's upper arm and pulled. He pulled again, harder. However much force he used he could not get him to move, and he began to be frightened he might dislocate his arm. He backed away, and Bernard Gidman took over.

Bernard tried to lift him, on the basis that the easiest way to get him out, was the way he had fallen in. But his head was jammed so tightly there was no movement in that direction either. Bernard was worried his skull had been fractured. Baffled and depressed, the two squeezed themselves back up the fissure to the surface to work out what to do next.

It was now after five o'clock. Gavin had been trapped for five and a half hours. They all knew there was little time left.

Peter Hurley picked up a zip gun – a compressed air chisel – and wriggled down into the hole that led to Gavin. As he disappeared, Robin Richards yelled down after him, 'Give him a bloody good yank.'

Peter had a much more delicate operation in mind. As carefully as he could, he started chipping away around the back and sides of Gavin's head. It was a dangerous thing to do; one slip could have injured or even killed him. It was easier when you knew there was no alternative.

An artist's impression of how Gavin was trapped, prepared for a Staffordshire Fire and Rescue Service incident report

He had been working on his knees for several minutes and was just starting to widen the gap at the back of the boy's head. The zip gun was in his right hand. With his left, he gave Gavin a little tug under his armpit. For the first time he felt him move. He threw the zip gun into the chasm and pulled with both arms, and out he came. Sweet and easy, like 'spreading butter in the summer'.

He pivoted, and leaned back to pass him over his body to Bernard who was crouching behind him. Brilliant, he thought, just brilliant.

Bernard lifted Gavin, and pushed him out through the entrance into the open air. At once, he was swept up and held above the crowd. What began as a shout of surprise, turned into prolonged cheering. People started to cry.

Dawn was pacing up and down by the police car at the bottom of the hill when a man ran past, yelling, 'He's out, he's out!' Seconds later, an ambulance drove past with its lights flashing. She jumped back into the police car and they followed the ambulance to the hospital.

Back on the hillside, the rescuers were reacting differently to the sudden release of tension and stress. Robin Richards felt like dancing now the burden of responsibility, not just for Gavin's life but for all the rescue team, had been lifted from his shoulders.

Bernard Gidman suddenly needed to be alone. He sat down on

'He lifted Gavin and pushed him out through the entrance into the open air. At once he was swept up and held above the crowd ... People started to cry'

a steep bank a hundred yards from the rescue site, and cried.

Mick Cape felt a sense of total exhilaration and wanted to hug everybody he saw. 'It was like scoring the winning goal for England.'

Peter Hurley was coming to terms with the success of the rescue more slowly. An hour before he had gone down with his zip gun for the final effort to free Gavin, he had decided the boy 'didn't have an earthly'. He had tried hard not to look at him as a person; tried hard not to get personally involved.

It was not until two days later that his emotions caught up with him. He was working under his car when his wife came out and starting reading a newspaper article about the rescue. 'I just couldn't come out from under the car. I just burst into tears.'

It was only as they helped to clear up the site that they fully realized just what risks they had run. As they pulled away the planks that had shored up the entrance, one fell into the hole. They listened for a long time as it fell, but they never heard it hit the bottom.

Then, as they moved more of the shoring away, the sides of the hole suddenly folded in as if they had turned to liquid. Bernard looked up at Peter and said what both of them thought: 'We wouldn't have had a cat in hell's chance.'

Bernard went to see Gavin in hospital. He was sitting up in bed in a side ward. The side of his head was swollen, and there were monitors attached to him. But he was well, and surprisingly cheerful.

He remembers little of his ordeal now. He has a collection of newspaper cuttings and television videos about his escape; and he has the fireman's helmet the firemen gave him afterwards, and a lamp from the mine rescue service.

A year later Bernard Gidman, Peter Hurley and Mick Cape went to Buckingham Palace to receive the Queen's Gallantry Medal for what they had done that day. The palace authorities took the unusual step of sending them in together for the presentation. Outside the gallery where it was to take place, a chamberlain gave them a rehearsal, walking them through the choreography of a royal presentation.

He met them again as they were leaving. 'You did brilliantly,' he said, 'even better than the last joint presentation we had.

'And they were Torvill and Dean.'

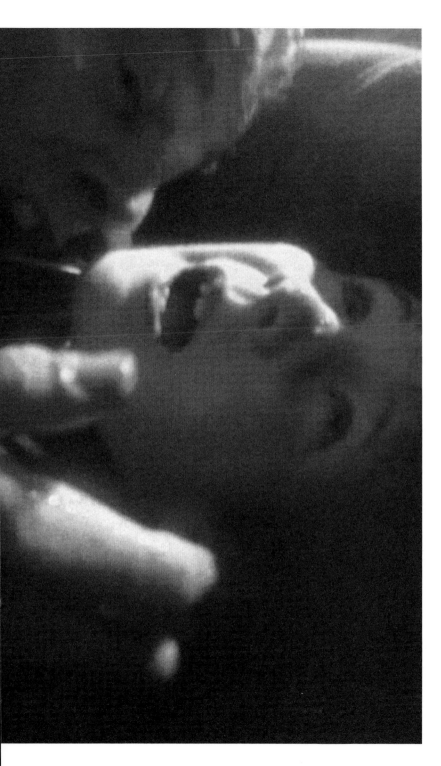

CHAPTER 14

Face in the Water

An accident can happen in a fraction of a second, but live in the minds of those involved for the rest of their lives. Even people who, by a miracle, survive unharmed constantly find themselves dwelling on what might have been. They need to share their story; bring their trauma out into the light, not bury it in the boxrooms of the brain to fester and destroy.

'There was a problem. He hated putting his face in the water. It was stopping him making progress'

It happened to Bruce Fowler in circumstances so ironic as to increase his sense of guilt. He so nearly killed his young son, Gary – and himself – within sight of his home and the rest of his family. It is something he has had to live with, and come to terms with, in the months that have followed.

Bruce is a serious, sensitive, intelligent man. He wrote to us because he felt telling people what happened would not only help him and his family to put the experience behind them, but also because it might achieve something positive out of what was, by any standards, a dreadful event.

Bruce and Gary went to the swimming pool at Ilkley every Monday night. Gary was six, and learning to swim. Normally, Bruce would go into the deep end of the pool, while Gary had his lesson down at the shallow end. But it was January; the weather had been bitterly cold, and Bruce decided he would give the water a miss that night. Ironic, in view of what was to happen later.

Gary was doing pretty well. He got his Watermanship award that night, and was working towards the five-metre badge, but there was a problem. He hated putting his face in the water. It was stopping him making progress.

They talked about it a little while Bruce helped Gary change. They were close then, and because of what they went through that night, are even closer now.

Out in the car park, Bruce spent quite a time fastening Gary into his special car seat. He and his wife Mary had become obsessive about seat belts ever since they had seen *That's Life* on BBC Television demonstrate what happened to children in a car crash when they were not wearing them. The dummies were crushed, thrown through windscreens, even run over. Ever since then they had spent a small fortune on harnesses for their two cars, changing them as Gary, and their younger son, Ben, grew bigger.

It was a short drive home, back down the Denton Road that ran alongside the River Wharfe. Their house was on the opposite bank of the river. Their route, that night and every Monday night, took them past the house, to a bridge which they crossed to double back to their home where Mary would have tea waiting. She would leave the curtains open, so they could see her working in the kitchen as they passed.

Bruce knew every inch of the road, and every inch of that part of the river too. As a child he had played there all the time. He had caught fish there, made dams, splashed around and learned to swim. He had seen the river in all its moods, even swollen and angry as it was that night. There had been heavy rain down in Ilkley and snow up in the Dales that had pushed the river up over its banks and across the road a day or so before. Now, the weather had cleared and the waters had receded a little. But they were still fierce and fast, and full of debris.

The radio had been on when Bruce had started the car, but he turned it down to talk to Gary about his problem with getting his face wet. Perhaps he would improve things if he splashed his face more in the shower, or in the bath. They reached the point in the road where they could see their house, and both looked up to see if Mary or Ben was in the window. Then it happened.

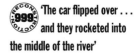

'The car flipped over . . . and they rocketed into the middle of the river'

As Bruce glanced back, his headlights picked up a flood warning sign that had been left there from a couple of days earlier. It was way out into the road, and he turned and braked to avoid it. He was a safe, defensive driver, who had never had so much as a parking ticket in twenty-three years behind the wheel. But the road was already greasy, and a couple of tractors had been along, making it even worse.

The car immediately went into an uncontrollable skid. It swerved sideways, across the white line, up and over a low wall, and down the river bank. For a split second, Bruce saw a bench he could see from his house across the water, and thought it might stop them. But the car flipped over, the bench disappeared, and they rocketed into the middle of the river.

It was the noise that brought Bruce round. He couldn't tell how long he had been unconscious, but he woke to the sound of roaring water everywhere. He was in darkness, still strapped into his seat; upside-down and drowning. His mouth was full of water. He did not know how much he had already swallowed. He thought he was going to die.

Mary had nearly finished preparing the tea, and was wondering where they had got to. She hadn't heard the crash. She was totally unaware that only seventy yards from her kitchen window her husband and son were fighting for their lives. If she had looked out she might have seen the wheels of their car sticking up out of the river. Instead she began to feel irritated. Bruce must have stopped to talk to the others at the pool, she thought. Typical. She started to put out the meal on the plates because they surely couldn't be much longer, and they'd be ravenous when they arrived.

'They were, he says, the worst moments of his life. Even now he can remember everything that went through his mind. Total recall of the living nightmare'

Down below, Bruce struggled with the seat belt, but couldn't find the catch. He fought to get his head out of the water. After moments that seemed like hours, he managed to lean across and, by bracing his body with his feet against the roof, push his head into an air pocket in the footwell on the passenger side of the car.

He gulped in the air, but knew it wouldn't last. The car was filling up with water. It was freezing cold and bringing him back to full consciousness. It was then he remembered Gary.

They were, he says, the worst moments of his life. Even now he can remember everything that went through his mind. Total recall of the living nightmare.

'It's impossible to describe,' he says, 'how horrifying it was.

'Gary was close to me in the darkness. I could hear gurgling noises from the back. I could tell he was drowning, but we were both trapped and there seemed nothing I could do.

'I thought we were both going to die. It was a question of who was going to die first. If I died first then that incredibly lovely, brave little boy was going to know that his dad was dead in the front of the car, and was going to be all alone. That was terrifying.'

That was when the guilt began.

'It was instant; the guilt that I, of all people, should have been the one to put him in the river, upside-down in the freezing water in January. It was impossible to bear.'

Bruce wriggled around a bit more and got an arm into the back of the car. He felt what he thought was Gary's coat and lifted it out of the water, only to find it was his legs. Then he managed to find his face, and pulled that towards him.

His head came up fairly easily. He coughed and spluttered for a moment and then said, very calmly, 'Are we in the river, Dad?'

'Yes, love, we are. But I'll get you out. It just might take a little while.'

But how? Here was this child who, a few minutes ago, couldn't bear to have water splashed into his face talking to him so calmly while they were both trapped upside-down under a raging river. He didn't even consider his dad wouldn't be able to get him out.

The throbbing from the gash on his head was nothing compared with the pain of thinking that they were not going to survive. Neither could move. He thought he was probably going to hold Gary's head out of the water until one of them died. They couldn't live long. The water was rising all the time. It was mostly melted snow off the Dales. The cold would kill them soon, if they did not drown first.

He wondered how people would cope. Especially Mary and Ben if the two of them were found dead in the car just opposite the house.

Again and again he tried to get his seat belt off, but he just could not find the catch. He was sure that without the belts they would both have died in the impact of the crash. The belts had saved their lives, but now they were killing them.

They had a few, brief conversations. He asked Gary if he was still OK. Each time he replied, 'Yes, Daddy.' Somehow his calmness kept Bruce from panicking.

Above the noise of the river they heard a car engine, and the lights from its headlamps swept briefly across the black water. For a moment their spirits rose. But there was a low wall between the road and the river. The driver couldn't see them, and drove on. Another car came and went. They realized they were completely alone; there was little hope of rescue.

There were moments of stillness and silence. Beautiful moments, Bruce thought. This is what it must be like to die.

But there were other moments, too. Moments when the anger and frustration welled up inside him. It was the anger that he harnessed into one last burst of energy. And it was the anger that saved him.

He remembers shouting out loud, 'God help me get this kid out of the car!' He wrenched himself from side to side and pushed his arms into every part of the car he could possibly reach, searching for the mountings on the seat belts.

Just when his anger, and his strength, was starting to ebb, he found them. He felt his way along until he came to the catch. At last he'd reached it. He released the catch, and twisted out of the belt. Seconds later, he was in the back of the car with Gary and wrestling with his harness, which was twisted up underneath him.

Soon they were both free, but only up to a point. They were still trapped inside the car. The roof had been crushed and the doors would not open. The water was backed up inside and the amount of air left seemed smaller and smaller. Also, it was rocking around in the floodwaters and Bruce was worried that it would be swept downriver. There were deep pools there, particularly when the river was this high. He had seen vehicles that had fallen into the river taken considerable distances and totally submerged. If that happened, he thought, they would have no chance.

He had to find a way out.

He noticed that the water was flowing through the car from the back, and started to feel round to see exactly where it was coming in. Several times he ducked under the black, filthy water to grope around the parcel shelf and the rear window. He discovered the tailgate was badly damaged and its window shattered.

For the first time, he thought they had a chance.

He told Gary what he was going to do. Then he ducked right down under the water and half swam, half hauled his way through the broken window.

He just hoped his legs would work. He was exhausted and in pain. He didn't know how badly injured he was. Everything would depend on whether he was able to stand up on the river bottom, in the swirling current. He pushed himself up out of the water, put

his feet down, and leant forward into the rush of the water.

He could do it. They might live after all.

Quickly he forced his way back into the car, and grabbed Gary by his coat, which had gathered up round his neck, and hauled him bodily through the back window. He got his feet on the river bed and stood upright, cuddling Gary close as he pulled him out of the water. He started to wade to the bank, and then stopped.

Maybe it was the relief, maybe some deeper emotion. But he can still vividly remember holding Gary up to the moon and the stars, and shrieking with ecstasy.

His only thought was: 'I put him in, but I got him out.'

Then slowly, painfully, overcome with desperate weariness, he started once more for the riverbank.

The accident had not gone unnoticed. The Fowlers' neighbour, Ian Campbell, had heard the crash and called for an ambulance. He realized who it was and headed up the road.

The first Mary knew anything was wrong was a knock at the door. Ian did not waste words.

'Bruce is in the river,' he said. 'Just down there, by the stepping stones. Follow me.'

It was as if she had been hit in the stomach. She grabbed hold of Ben and pushed him into the car. They roared off down the road to the bridge and all the time she was thinking, 'He only mentioned Bruce. What's happened to Gary?'

Even now, she can remember how it felt like a hundred years before she reached the bridge and turned to come back up the other bank to the stepping stones. Ahead of her she could see the ambulance.

Bruce had reached the side of the river, just as Ian Campbell's wife, Janet, got there. They knew each other well. Janet was Gary's playschool teacher. He handed him over to her, and collapsed back into the river, finally overcome with exhaustion.

She yelled at him, worried he would be swept away. After a few moments, she managed to grab hold of his hand and pull him out of the water.

By then the ambulance had arrived. Bruce and Gary were both taken into the back of it and wrapped in space blankets to counter the cold and exposure. That was how Mary found them. The expression on her face when she saw Gary, and realized he wasn't dead, is one more thing about that night Bruce can never forget.

Bruce was bleeding badly from the wound on his head. Gary was just cold and frightened. They were both shocked and dazed.

Gary can remember lying in the ambulance and seeing the trees flashing past in the darkness out of the top of the windows. But, by the time he had reached the hospital, he was recovering fast. As he was lying on the trolley waiting to go into X-ray he even started joshing his father about what had happened. 'Really, Daddy,' he said, 'you shouldn't try to wash the car in the river.'

It was not going to be so easy for Bruce. He was already suffering from the trauma that he is maybe only now coming to terms with, years later. He couldn't believe Gary was still alive, and needed to be reassured he was OK every few minutes. And, even though they had survived, he was crippled with guilt.

Normally, the hospital would have kept Bruce in for the night, but they decided to let him go home with Gary. It was a sensitive and wise decision. That night he kept getting up, every twenty minutes or so, and walking up the stairs to Gary's bedroom. He needed to see him, to hold him, to prove to himself, over and over again, he hadn't been killed.

The next day, they decided it was important for Gary to get back to normal as soon as possible. They took him into school, only a little later than the proper starting time. Even then Bruce had to go to the school when they were having their break to make sure Gary was still safe.

All he could think of was how children expect their parents to look after them, and depend on them completely. Gary's total faith that his father would get them both out had driven Bruce to desperate efforts when they were trapped, but now, somehow, seemed to add to his guilt at getting him into that situation in the first place.

Bruce Fowler with his sons Gary (right) and Ben, who 'feel stronger as a family, and live each day more fully, after having experienced the feeling that they had seen their last'

Mary remembers Bruce needed a lot of support, in that first week after the accident. Every time he looked out of the window he was reminded they could have died a few yards from their own back door while Mary made their tea. Worse, how close they were to being completely trapped. If the back window had not been broken they would just have had to hold each other, and wait for the first to die.

The car stayed in the river for a few days, its wheels sticking up out of the receding floodwaters. Mary was glad when they took it away. It sent a chill down her spine every time she saw it. She could never really understand how they had escaped.

Bruce and Gary found the remains of the windscreen further downstream. Between them they retrieved the tax disc, and reclaimed £60 from the licensing authorities.

It took a long time before Bruce could bring himself to tell Gary off, for anything. But, unfortunately for Gary, that wore off as Bruce began to get over the worst of his trauma. They have all managed to find something positive out of such a dreadful experience. They feel stronger as a family, they live each day more fully, after having experienced the feeling that they had seen their last.

Bruce campaigns now for the greater use of seat belts. Being trapped underwater, as he was, is one of the main arguments used against seat belts. He looks at it differently. You've always got a chance of releasing the harness, he says. But you can't if you have been killed by the impact because you were not wearing one.

As for Gary, he has brought something positive from that night, too. Apart from anything else, he's no longer worried about getting his face in the water.

How to Escape from a Sinking Car

Over the last five years (1989–1993) 136 people have drowned in Britain, trapped in their vehicles. That means every year more people drown this way than in boating accidents. These incidents happen when wet roads, flash floods and freak waves can sweep cars into rivers or the sea but human error is often a factor too.

What you can do
Plunging into deep, dark water is a frightening experience, but if it happens to you, try not to panic. The inside of a family car will hold a large enough air bubble for you to breathe while you prepare to escape. Your car will float for a few seconds after hitting the water. In these first vital moments you should free yourself and all your passengers from seat belts and child safety harnesses. Use as little effort as possible to conserve the air in the car and try and keep everyone's heads above the water level as it begins to rise.

Wind down your windows before the car sinks. This might seem like the most terrifying thing to do as

water pours in, but until the water pressure is the same on both the inside and outside it will be very difficult to open the doors. If your car has electric windows they're unlikely to work under water.

Blow bubbles to indicate the direction of the surface and although it will be against your instincts, you need to push the doors wide open. Make sure you help any children and older people out first. It's safest to stick together, so try and hold hands to form a human chain and swim to the surface. Even if you are in a soft-topped car or a car with a sunroof you should still make every effort to get out through the doors not the roof, as the clips

may be stuck or the space too small to wriggle through. You may waste valuable time, and air, trying to get out this way.

● Free yourself and the other passengers from seatbelts and child safety harnesses.
● Use as little effort as possible to conserve air.
● Keep everyone's heads above the water as it rises in the car.
● Wind down the windows to equalize pressure.
● Open doors gently. Push them wide open and get out.
● To make sure that everyone reaches safety, hold hands and form a human chain and swim to the surface together.

The Life Hammer
We know how difficult it was for Bruce to release his seat belt underwater and how lucky it was that the back window of the car shattered on impact, providing a vital escape route. But what would have happened if the seat belt had jammed or the window had remained intact? Several *999* viewers have written to us about a special tool called a Life Hammer which they carry with them in their cars after similar accidents. It's a combination of a hammer (for breaking windows) and a sharp blade (for cutting through seat belts).

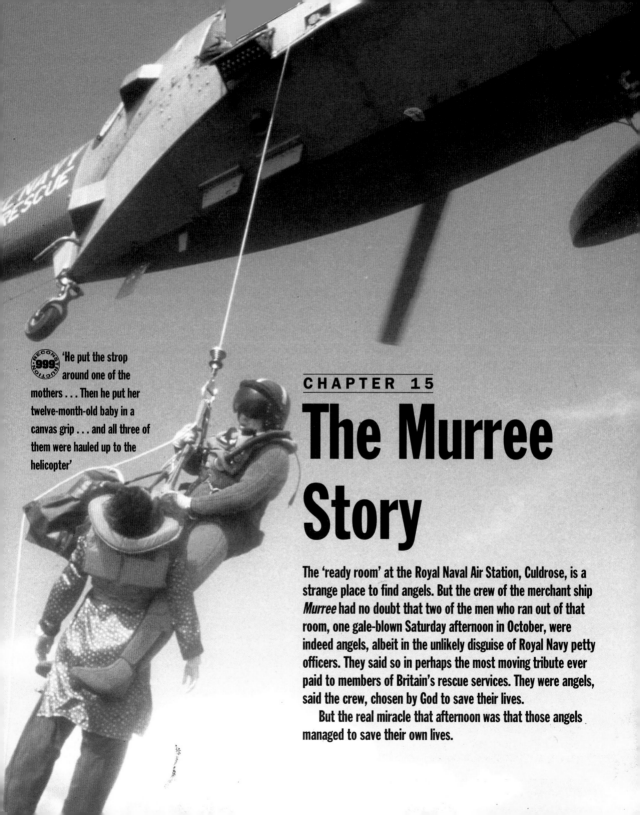

'He put the strop around one of the mothers . . . Then he put her twelve-month-old baby in a canvas grip . . . and all three of them were hauled up to the helicopter'

CHAPTER 15

The Murree Story

The 'ready room' at the Royal Naval Air Station, Culdrose, is a strange place to find angels. But the crew of the merchant ship *Murree* had no doubt that two of the men who ran out of that room, one gale-blown Saturday afternoon in October, were indeed angels, albeit in the unlikely disguise of Royal Navy petty officers. They said so in perhaps the most moving tribute ever paid to members of Britain's rescue services. They were angels, said the crew, chosen by God to save their lives.

But the real miracle that afternoon was that those angels managed to save their own lives.

A lot of what goes on in the search and rescue ready room is routine. It is a big room, maybe thirty feet long. One whole wall is covered by a map of the area the helicopters cover, with their base, on the Lizard in Cornwall, at its centre. On another wall there is a bank of telephones, connecting them with the other rescue services. The crackle and chatter of an open radio line to the coastguard is permanently on in the background. It is full of chairs; there is a television and an endless supply of tea and coffee. A waiting room for angels.

One crew is always on duty, another on standby, wearing their bleepers and no more than an hour and a half away. The shifts last twenty-four hours. There is a lot of paperwork to do, plenty of studying to work through. Even when there is no emergency, they get airborne for an hour and a half a day on training exercises. Once a week they do a night flight.

But, for twenty-four hours at a time, that room is the centre of their lives. At night, they sleep next door. In the summer they play volleyball outside. At the weekends, their families come in. The crew's job is to be there, waiting for the phone to ring.

Steve Wright had not expected to be working that weekend. His opposite number on the duty crew was a keen rugby player whose club, Helston, had a key match that afternoon. Steve volunteered to cover for him. His mates called him 'Shiner'. Nicknames are traditional in the navy and every Wright since Trafalgar has been called Shiner. A good name for an angel, when you think about it.

They called Dave Wallace 'Wally', but he had been called that ever since he was a child. He had finished his duty shift that morning and was on standby, hoping for a quiet afternoon.

Shiner and Wally were point men for the rescue crews. When it came to lowering somebody on the end of the helicopter winch to sort out the emergency, they were the ones who had to do it. Originally, their main job was to rescue pilots whose planes had gone over the side of aircraft carriers, and they are still trained as divers. That training probably saved both their lives before the afternoon was over.

It was a wild day, the worst that autumn. Violent gales funnelled in from the South Western Approaches, stripping the trees of their remaining leaves and beating the sea into dark valleys and dirty foam.

It was no day to be afloat, even on a ship as large as the Murree. The Pakistani freighter had left Antwerp bound for Karachi the previous night, the decks crowded with containers and the quarters packed with people. Thirty-six men, two women and two small children were on board her that afternoon as she took on the sea, and lost.

Nobody will ever know now how it happened, but some time that morning, as the ship smashed head-on through waves more than twenty feet high, the cargo started to shift. One container must have come loose and started putting pressure on those next to it. By the time the crew noticed, there was nothing anybody could do. The ship was doomed.

Steve Wright came on at midday, and settled into the ready room as his opposite number changed out of his flying overalls and picked up his rugby gear. There had already been a flurry of calls because of the bad weather, but nothing had yet turned into a full-scale emergency. They listened to the coastguard radio for the first signs of serious trouble. It was much busier than normal. Outside, the wind shrieked across the airfield, the sort of day when the search and rescue crews earn their money.

The first call came through just before three o'clock. It was Brixham coastguard putting them on alert to help a freighter in difficulties just off Start Point on the Devon coast. The duty crew was always ready for an immediate scramble that would have them airborne within three and a half minutes. But that is only in life and death situations, relatively close to the base. Most of their operations are cleared through the Rescue Co-ordination Centre in Plymouth, and they get a bit of warning. Steve wondered whether to change into his wet suit then, or wait until he was in the helicopter. It made you sweat so much, most divers left it until the last moment. He decided to wait.

Twenty minutes later the Rescue Co-ordination Centre called them on the red scramble telephone and ordered them to fly to the aid of the Murree. The details were scanty and, it turned out, wrong. Radio communication with the freighter had been difficult. The ship's officers knew they were in trouble, but not how serious it really was. Most crucial of all, the coastguards were not able to catch how many were on board. They told the navy men it was either

> '**Outside, the wind shrieked across the airfield, the sort of day when the search and rescue crews earn their money**'

four or fourteen people that had to be taken off. As the crew of the Sea King HAR 5 warmed up the engines and strapped themselves in they had no idea they would have to rescue forty people, and that time was already running out.

Just over half an hour later they were over the *Murree*, bouncing in the turbulence with the gale gusting between sixty and seventy-five miles an hour. It was immediately obvious to all of them that the ship was in a bad way. The huge containers were breaking off the front deck like matchboxes, and the ship itself was taking on water in the heavy seas. It had already begun to settle down by the bows. The two pilots brought the Sea King into the hover and started to slide sideways through the gusts towards the ship. The winch operator helped Steve hook himself on and, when they were directly over the stern, lowered him down.

On the ship it was all much worse than Steve had expected. There was so much confusion, so many people, and not just men, but women and babies too. Communication was the first problem. Many did not understand English but, by doing a lot of shouting, waving his arms about and giving people angry looks he managed

'Just over half an hour later they were over the *Murree*. It was immediately obvious to all of them that the ship was in a bad way. It had already begun to settle down by the bows'

to get them to do what he wanted. The next problem was getting the women and children off first. The two wives did not want to leave their husbands, who were senior officers and insisting that they, themselves, should leave last. If they were to die, the women said, they wanted to die with their men.

Steve's sense of urgency broke through the language barriers, and the crew forced them to go.

Getting the children up took time. He put the strop around one of the mothers, and hooked the D-ring on to the winch. Then he put her twelve-month-old baby in a canvas grip that his flying gear was normally packed in. He zipped it up to stop any risk of the child falling out and then hooked himself on to the winch and all three of them were hauled up to the helicopter.

The second child was eighteen months old, and much larger than the first, so he got a bigger bag for him and took him up on his own. Then he went up again with the child's mother.

He breathed a bit easier with the women and children safe, but there were still three dozen men on board. The weather was getting worse and he could feel, from the motion of the ship beneath his feat, that she would not last for long. He wondered then if there would be enough time to get everybody off.

He did not know if he would have the strength, either. Each winching operation took its toll of his energy, as he fought to drag the hook across to the ship. It was impossible for the helicopter to maintain position directly overhead. It had to be slightly to one side of it so that the pilots could see it more clearly, and have the constant visual reference they needed to keep the aircraft steady. That meant that they were winching the hook down some distance from the ship, and Steve had to haul it across to the deck on a 250-foot rope they called the hi-line. Each time, the gale plucked at the line and tried to tear it out of his hands. He was getting the crew off, two at a time, but it was exhausting.

He wondered how long it would be before they sent help.

Dave Wallace could not remember a gale like it. He had gone out to walk the dog that afternoon around the village of Cury where he lived and it was difficult enough just standing up. He had taken the dog up on to the playing fields to watch the local football team. The goalkeeper tried to take a goal kick into the gale, but the wind blew it back over the line for a corner. The winger was just coming up to take it when Dave's bleeper went off.

He ran all the way back to the house, and when he got there the Culdrose operator was already on the phone. There was no time to change. Just a quick kiss for his wife, Carol, in the usual pandemonium of his rushed departures. The kids were yelling and the dog was barking itself hoarse as he jumped into the car, still in his jeans and boots, for the fast, three-mile drive to the base.

When he got to the ready room the two pilots were having trouble finding a winch operator. The regular member of the crew was not answering his bleeper. It turned out he had gone shopping at a DIY superstore in Falmouth, and the metal framework of the building blocked out the electronic signal. It was not his fault, but he was not popular as they rang round trying to find a replacement. Eventually they tracked down Nigel Toms, a winch operator with one of the crews that was off-watch, and he agreed to come in. Dave Wallace was already in his orange wet suit when the last of the team arrived and they were able to head off for the Murree.

The crews call their helicopters 'cabs'. Three of them were sent to the Murree that afternoon. Steve Wright's 'cab' had gone with a full load of thirteen people back to Plymouth, leaving him still on board. When Dave Wallace and his team arrived there was a Mark IV Sea King from the navy base at Portland lifting off more of the crew, and they circled waiting for it to finish. The Mark IV can carry more people than the later version that operates out of Culdrose. They managed to pack seventeen men off the Murree into the helicopter before it, too, headed for the shore.

From the air they could see how quickly the Murree was foundering. The bows were being swamped by huge waves. Each one seemed to reach further up the stump mast at the front of the ship than the last. As they winched him down to the deck, Dave Wallace knew there was not much time left. He did not know that time would be measured in minutes.

Steve was glad to see him. 'Thank Christ you're here,' he said, 'I'm knackered,' and he looked it. Ten of the ship's crew were left on board. There had been some panic when Steve had first arrived, but now those that remained were calm and formed an orderly queue across the narrow stern deck.

Steve asked Dave to take over the winching operation, so that he could go forward to the bridge to radio the coastguard. The pilots had been passing information to the people on shore, but Steve knew he was the only person who could give them a full situation report on the rescue, and the state of the ship.

Dave had managed to lift another four of the crew up into the helicopter by the time Steve got back. He was looking worried. He had managed to contact the coastguard at Brixham all right but it was what he could see while he was speaking to them that brought home to him for the first time how dangerous the situation had become. Until then, he had been too preoccupied with the lifting operation to take much notice and, in any case, the bridge had blocked off his view of the bow of the ship.

'We'll have to get a shift on,' he told Dave. 'It's murder up there.' He had seen the bows covered in white water, surf roaring along the deck, boiling and bubbling towards them. Up there, out of the howling wind, he could hear rumbling noises from below decks, as the Murree took in more and more water. The coastguard had finished by saying, 'Good luck, boys' in a way that Steve thought meant he felt they would need it. They would and all.

As they helped the next two on to the winch they talked of what they should do. They decided they would both stay until they had got everybody off. That way, if the ship went down they would only have each other to worry about.

Those two reached the helicopter. Four to go now. They only needed ten more minutes. They were not going to get it.

They were fitting the next two into the strops when there was an explosion under their feet. Some of the bulkheads down below had given way. The deck pitched upwards, almost throwing them off their feet. A long, rumbling noise told them the seawater was filling up the hull. Two to go.

For a few moments they thought they were going to get away with it. They fitted the canvas loops round the captain and the second

> ‘"We'll have to get a shift on," he told Dave. "It's murder up there."’

officer, and watched impatiently as the winch pulled them away from the deck. The last two members of the *Murree*'s crew were on their way. Dave and Steve had done their job, now all they had to do was save themselves. The two crewmen had just reached the door of the helicopter, and Nigel Toms was furiously trying to free the hook to send it back down, when there was a second explosion, louder than the first, and they knew they had left it too late.

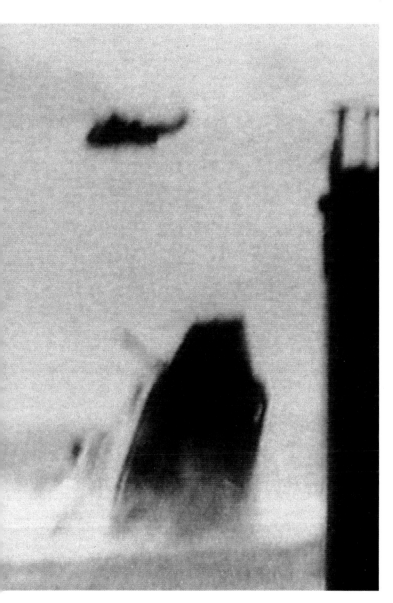

It was the biggest bang Dave had ever heard. It was the last bulkheads giving way, in the stern immediately beneath them. The ship was finished. There was a rolling thunder as thousands more gallons of seawater poured in, and the great stern of the ship reared up out of the sea.

The two divers clung on the back rail, both swearing mightily. They signalled up to the helicopter to speed up the winch, but Nigel Toms already knew he would not be able to get the wire back in time. He could see the bows of the ship going down; it was sinking in front of his eyes. The hi-line was snagging in the wreckage on the deck, slowing the winch down. The hook was only halfway back to them, when Nigel leaned out of the helicopter and, with unmistakable gestures, told them they would have to jump.

'These were its death throes. The stern went straight up, almost to vertical. It was heading for the bottom'

Dave turned to Steve and said, 'This is it, mate. We're going to have to go for it.' Something made him add, 'See you on the other side' – which he thought later covered all eventualities. In truth, neither thought they would live more than another few minutes. They let go to move over to the port side of the ship, when it lurched again. These were its death throes. The stern went straight up, almost to vertical. It was heading for the bottom.

Dave and Steve were thrown across the deck, crashing into the capstan heads, bouncing off the superstructure. Steve managed to hang on to a bollard; Dave was stopped by a rope that got tangled up round his ankle. He was busy unwrapping it when Steve reached the guard rail, paused only for a second and jumped over. His mind was full of goodbyes: to his wife, to his family, to his mates on the squadron. He did not think he would see any of them again.

Dave looked up to see Steve's head disappearing over the side, and the water boiling up the deck towards him. He got to the rail in time to see Steve hit the water far below. If there had been any alternative he would not have jumped. It was the equivalent of throwing himself off a ten-storey block of flats. The height itself was dangerous, and the water was full of massive containers and other wreckage. If he hit any of it he would not have to worry about drowning; he would be dead before he reached the water.

He ripped off his flying helmet – if it got caught on the way down it would have taken his head off. He quickly looked over his shoulder to see if the propellers were turning and was momentarily relieved to see they had stopped. Any death was preferable to being chewed up by a ship's screws. He looked for a clear spot in the water, found one, took a deep breath and jumped.

It took an hour to reach the water, or at least it felt that way. He kept his arms and feet straight, the way he practised every week. But practice jumps were never more than twenty feet. The helicopter crew that was watching was able to make an accurate assessment of the height they both jumped, and reckoned it was more than ninety feet. He smashed into the water and kept on going.

His eyes were open and he saw the water change colour as he drove down into it. Frothy white on the surface, then green, then darker green and finally black, and then he could not see anything any more. He was wearing an aircrew lifejacket, but that would not inflate if it was more than eight yards below the surface, and he was far deeper than that. After what seemed like another hour, he stopped sinking and started to rise back towards the surface. He began to see colour in the water again. He looked over his right shoulder and there was the ship, sliding past him on its way to the seabed. He could see the rust streaks along its sides and felt he had only to reach out to be able to touch the hull as it passed by. Its huge gravity tugged at him and he felt the sharp fear of being dragged down with it, of being sucked to the bottom to share its grave.

The lifejacket suddenly gave a pop, and started to inflate with a long sigh, pulling him to the surface. The first thing he saw when he got there was the stern of the ship, big as a tower block, still looming above him and only about ten yards away. It was all in black and white, like an old film about the *Titanic*. Even the debris was huge. The containers, vast boxes being banged together by the waves. Great chunks of metal that had been ripped from the deck. He felt so small, so weak and powerless.

He was overwhelmed by self-pity. He was convinced he was going to die. He said out loud, 'Sorry, Carol, I've blown it this time,' and there was a lump in his throat as he thought of never seeing the children again.

Perhaps it was the thought of them that got him going. One moment he was resigned to dying; the next he was saying 'Bugger that' at the top of his voice and swimming like a good 'un to get away from the ship. He let the air out of his lifejacket and kicked off his training shoes so that he could go faster, driven on by the terror of being sucked back down under water. He turned on to his back for a moment, in time to catch a last sight of the very stern of the *Murree* slip beneath the waves. Even then he did not stop swimming, he still thought the sinking ship would drag him down with it.

He was still swimming furiously when there was a moment of magic. From nowhere, a hook appeared in front of him. For the second time in as many minutes he was close to crying.

Nigel Toms had watched both men jump, and seen the plumes of water as they hit the sea. He saw the first one come back to the surface but by then he was working to free the winch wire and did not see the other until the helicopter was directly over him. Nigel had cut through the hi-line, and was now able to dangle the hook in front of the diver, almost like fishing for a trout.

Dave had enough strength left to hook himself on and Nigel started to winch him up. When he was just clear of the water he spun himself round and caught sight of Steve, floating nearby. He signalled to Nigel and the helicopter moved across so that he could grab him.

Steve had hurt himself quite badly, though he did not realize it at the time. He lost his balance as he fell, and waved his arms about trying to regain it. His arms were above his head as he hit the water with enormous force, and the impact ripped all the tendons in his right shoulder. He was still able to attach his harness to the winch and give Dave a cuddle as they were hoisted up to the aircraft.

They can both remember screaming with the relief, so loud they were surprised the people in the helicopter did not hear them. They hugged each other and yelled, 'We made it,' over and over.

The first thing that hit them when they reached the door of the helicopter was the eyes of the last three or four of the Murree's crew that they had saved. Big as dinner plates, Dave thought. They had been sitting by the open door and they had seen it all. They had watched their ship suddenly tilt straight down. They had watched their rescuers throw themselves off the stern and told each other the two divers were dead. And now there they were, in the helicopter. There was a feeling of having witnessed something more than human. A feeling among them all, Muslim, Christian, agnostic, that some other power, greater than man's, had taken a hand.

As the helicopter headed back to shore, the Murree's second officer, Irfran Jafri, asked for a pen. All the ship's crew had been told to take off their bulky lifejackets, as a safety precaution so that they could get out of the helicopter quickly in an emergency. On the back of his, Irfran Jafri wrote a message of thanks. A message that eloquently summed up their gratitude, and their feelings at that emotional moment (*see right*).

They dropped the Murree crewmen off at RAF Mountbatten in Plymouth. There, Steve was able to rejoin his own aircraft. The

'To the angels who came in the guise of men. The Lord hath chosen thee to perform the most profound of his miracles — saving life. You are what the world was made for'

divers' day was not yet over. They just had time for Steve to have a quick cigarette and them both to gulp down half a cup of tea before they were scrambled twice more, in quick succession. They were sent to Dartmoor to investigate some emergency flares, which proved to be a false alarm. Then they had to rescue two people and a dog, trapped by the tide at the foot of a cliff in Plymouth Sound.

It was getting dark by the time they got back to Culdrose, and what they had done had still not sunk in.

Dave was supposed to be going to a Hallowe'en party in the mess that night, but he and Carol never made it. Instead he went to bed early. By midnight he realized he was never going to be able to sleep. He made himself something to eat and drink, then paced around the house until dawn, unable to settle down.

On Sunday he went in to the base and saw Steve, who had come out of the sick bay with his arm in a sling, and they went over it all again. That night, while he was watching television, Dave suddenly realized he was heavily bruised all down the side of his body; he still can't remember how he did it. The bruises faded quickly, but he reckons it took him a couple of months to get over the whole thing emotionally, and start sleeping normally again.

Dave and Steve were both awarded the George Medal, and a string of other prizes, for their courage. Parts of the rescue had been filmed from the air and the incident received wide publicity. It was the heart-felt message of thanks from Irfan Jafri that struck a chord with people, that made an extraordinary rescue somehow a symbol of the God-given potential of human nature. Dave had a card from Irfan a year

Dave Wallace (left) and Steve Wright who gave the crew of the stricken *Murree* the 'gift of life'

later, but there was no address on it. He has tried to contact him since without success.

Every so often he gets the lifejacket out of the box where he keeps it, and reads what is written on it again. It means a lot to him and, perhaps, sums up the feelings of so many people featured in this book towards those who rescued them, gave them a gift of life.

Post-traumatic Stress Disorder Information

Almost forty per cent of people who are in dreadful events will show a post-traumatic reaction, so too will five per cent of rescuers. That's about 600,000 people in the UK at any one time. It's not only national disasters like Hillsborough and King's Cross that leave people emotionally scarred, but personal tragedies too. Victims of car crashes, fires and near drownings are increasingly encouraged to seek treatment for post-traumatic stress disorder. And with help now available from the National Health Service, no one need suffer alone.

Symptoms

Many people who experience post-traumatic stress disorder have flashbacks – memories and images of a traumatic incident they just can't get out of their mind. A feeling of guilt is normal too. They may find it difficult to relax and often have trouble sleeping, resulting in exhaustion and depression. They may also feel very alone, unable to ask anyone for help. They avoid talking to people and visiting places that remind them of what happened.

It's important for family and friends to watch out for these symptoms. They may begin immediately after the trauma, or develop many months later. Most people recover, given time, emotional support and counselling. But early diagnosis and treatment are important. If the condition is not recognized, over half of all sufferers will go on to develop clinical depression and there is a marked increase in marital problems and risk of suicide.

Treatment

The treatment of post-traumatic stress disorder consists of counselling sessions and exposure therapy, encouraging the sufferer to relive and cope with memories of the incident and maybe even return to the place where it all actually happened.

It is not only those who are physically scarred who suffer this mental anguish. Those people who attend disasters – from the fire, police and ambulance services – are often affected too. At least five per cent of rescuers become victims themselves. They are often the ones who don't get the help they need, either because they feel ashamed that they can't cope in their job, or they may be afraid of any treatment that reminds them of the disaster itself. Most rescue services now offer confidential counselling and courses for their staff.

Where to get help on the NHS

Dr Thompson
The Stress Clinic
Middlesex Hospital
Wolfston Building
Riding House Street
London W1N 8AA

Dr H Noschirvani
Maudsley Hospital
99 Denmark Hill
London SE5 8AZ

and other local specialists recommended by your doctor.

INDEX